Famous Biographies for Young People

FAMOUS AMERICAN
HUMOROUS POETS

by Everett S. Allen

ILLUSTRATED WITH PHOTOGRAPHS

Dodd, Mead & Company · New York

I am particularly grateful for the assistance rendered by Miss Rita E. Steele, librarian, and her staff, of the Millicent Library in Fairhaven; Librarian Jack McMahon of the Boston Herald; Jack Simms, Associated Press chief of bureau, Boston; Charles W. Flagg, Wide World Photos, Inc., Boston; Samuel G. Blackman, general news editor, Associated Press, New York, and for the opportunity of using the files of the New Bedford (Mass.) Standard-Times, through the courtesy of James H. Ottaway Jr., publisher.

Library of Congress Catalog Card Number: 68-16178
Printed in the United States of America
by Vail-Ballou Press, Inc., Binghamton, N.Y.

FOREWORD

This book is for the young, but not exclusively, for, implicitly, it reveals the important relationship of laughter to life, and this is something of which we cannot be reminded too often.

The woodpecker, I am told, has some sort of cartilaginous shock absorber at the base of his bill so that he does not fracture his skull each time he hammers a tree trunk.

Automobiles have delicately balanced mechanisms that I do not pretend to understand, the function of which is to make the occupants unaware that they have just driven over a bump.

Roads and bridges are built with room for contraction and expansion due to temperature change, so that they will not buckle and fragment when harassed by the atmospheric vacillations from January to July.

This is the kind of service that humor provides for man. When his normally stubborn spirit is in danger of being sandpapered to within an inch of its life by adversity or frustration, he stands outside himself, as it were, and is moved to laughter at sight of his own ridiculousness. This process provides lubrication for the ego and prevents it from becoming arthritic, and therefore easily shatterable.

In the lives of some of these people, you will find tears as well as laughter but the two have never been far apart, and one often produces the other—and this I cannot help, and would not if I could, for that is the stuff (as Ogden Nash would say) of life.

The most disturbing sign herein is the feeling of several of the occupants that, as Americans, we do not write enough humor, read enough humor, or laugh enough. If this little book encourages some to improve the situation, it will have served a sufficient purpose.

Some may note that such old friends as Oliver Wendell Holmes, physician, essayist, anatomy professor, and the wittiest of the outstanding New England poets of his day, and Francis Bret Harte, author of the indestructible *Plain Language from Truthful James* might have been included. They were not because the effort has been to concentrate on writers closer to our own time. Further, it might be pointed out that this is not intended as an anthology (undoubtedly, your good librarian or bookseller would be pleased to recommend one or better still, the original volumes of the authors), but rather as a glimpse into the lives of some who have made us laugh, to suggest how this came about.

I shall not delay you longer. They are playing the overture. The curtain is about to rise. It is time for you to become acquainted with some very worthwhile people, and I hope you come to like them as much as I have.

EVERETT S. ALLEN

Poverty Point
Fairhaven, Massachusetts

CONTENTS

Illustrations follow page 64

To my father
JOSEPH CHASE ALLEN
who first introduced me to the works
of Don Marquis (which he memorized
by the yard); who has written humorous light verse for more than forty
years, including the following:

Warring World

With outright war and violence,
  The world has been disrupted since
My early childhood, and I wot
  That buried in some lonely spot
My grave will then be bulldozed, too,
  To let a superhighway through.

and who, finally, has im   pon
me since childhood the oc   al importance of not being earnest

E.S.A.

FRANKLIN PIERCE ADAMS

[1881–1960]

Franklin pierce adams has been described by a writer who admired him as being "attractively ugly," possessing the elongated features of an intelligent horse, and the warm eyes of a cocker spaniel. Many saw in his appearance a mustached resemblance to the comedian Groucho Marx and, more deeply, thousands found in Adams a remarkable mixture of erudition and common sense.

Principally known as "F.P.A.," Adams was born in Chicago on November 15, 1881, the son of Moses and Clara (Schlossberg) Adams. He attended the Stephen Douglas School, named for the nineteenth-century American political figure. F.P.A.'s recollections of these years are typical in their sprightly sensitivity:

"In the Douglas school, we had a bust of Stephen Douglas in the hall and there was nothing in the assembly room but pictures of Stephen Douglas, and I should say that it wasn't until I was in the eighth grade that I heard of Abe Lincoln. (With whom Douglas engaged in the famous debates on slavery in the 1850s.)"

Mr. Adams recalled, "I remember the first day I went to Douglas school. I remember it, I guess, because of a daily half-

9

hour we had in Miss Graham's room—Room 24. This is the kind of stuff I remember. The first thing we had was singing, and they had a song called, 'Where do all the daisies go? I know. I know.' There was another part that goes, 'In the springtime do they peep.' and then, 'Out they peep.'

"I didn't sing that song. I didn't like it. I was a fairly young man of 7. I thought that was quite a silly song. I still think so. [This reflection was voiced by F.P.A. at the age of 65.]

"I went to the University of Michigan to get away from home. I didn't know that while I was there, but I know it now. When you go away from home, you can stay up as late as you like. I was humiliated there by a Professor Dow, who asked me about the effect of some battle, so I thought I'd better let the University of Michigan shift for itself, and I am sorry to say that it has done so with conspicuous success."

After his one year at Michigan (which had been preceded by his graduation from the Armour Scientific Academy in 1899), Adams went looking for work. This is how he remembered the experience: "In Chicago, I found a job in the insurance profession. My job was to wrap up policies that were sent to the agents every month. Later, I was permitted to be an insurance solicitor, going around asking people, 'Don't you want insurance?' Some of them said yes, but not very many.

"My hero was a writer named George Ade [then a foremost American writer of humor]. I went around to where he lived at 11:30 o'clock on a February morning and I asked the door man at the athletic club if he was [sic] in. He said, 'Yes, he's in there having breakfast.' At 11:30 in the morning, he was having breakfast. At our house, if we weren't through breakfast at half past seven in the morning, there wasn't any breakfast.

"I went up to Mr. Ade and said, 'You don't want any insurance, do you?'"

Mr. Ade didn't, but as a result of this contact, Adams ceased selling insurance and turned to the career that was to make him famous. "It was 1903," F.P.A. later recalled, "and I had never written anything before, but I went over to the Chicago *Journal* and asked for a job writing a column. Mr. McKay, the editor, said, 'All right, sit down and write a column.'

"I worked on the paper quite a while and I used to go around and bother George Ade a good deal, showing him what I had written. After about a year of this, he said to me, 'If I were you, I would go to New York.' I still don't know whether he got sick of the sight of me or whether it was good advice. Well, if he had told me to jump off the editorial tower of the building, I would have done it. That was the extent of my hero worship. Sometimes I wish he had advised me to jump."

With occasional lapses, Adams' column appeared in New York daily newspapers from 1904 to the fall of 1941, including the *Evening Mail*, the *Tribune*,—in which it first appeared under the eventually famous title "The Conning Tower"—and in the *World*, *Herald-Tribune*, and the *Post*. Commenting on this period, F.P.A. said, "I went to New York and worked on various papers until they went out of business, either on account of me, or in spite of me." However, this is an extremely wry and modest summary of a very successful career.

On the *Journal*, at the outset of his newspaper work, young Adams was paid $25 a week; by 1937, he was being paid $21,852 a year for a syndicated column in the New

York *Herald-Tribune.*

The ingredients of this success were numerous and, in a few instances, unique.

F.P.A. once was described by a newspaper editorial writer as a man "who seems to know everything, from the whole score of Gilbert and Sullivan to the latest news of Turkey's neutrality, despite the fact that he never finished college. He must have picked up this dazzling array of information in the many newspaper offices that he has frequented. . . ." Yet Adams insisted that he never memorized a song or poem on purpose in his life, that they registered themselves in his memory through sheer rereading or rehearing through the years.

His quick and wide-ranging intellect attracted not only a reading audience—which reveled in F.P.A.'s own "Pepys' diary" of poker playing, reading, tennis, his punning and light verse—but also kindred creative spirits whose contributions to "The Conning Tower" (submitted gratis, in the custom of those times) founded both his success and theirs. Among these contributors were Dorothy Parker, George S. Kaufman, Deems Taylor, John O'Hara, Edna St. Vincent Millay, Arthur Guiterman, Sinclair Lewis, Ring Lardner, Edna Ferber.

Concerning this period, F.P.A. recalled, "There was a fellow I got a poem from once. I read it and told my wife, 'Here's a man with one poem in his system and he got it out. I'll never hear from him again.' I used it, and I'm glad to say I was wrong. His name is Ogden Nash."

During World War I, he was sent abroad to write "The Listening Post" column for the infant military newspaper *Stars and Stripes.* Before cleaning out his desk at the New York *Herald-Tribune,* he wrote in his weekly "Diary of Our

Own Samuel Pepys": "Early to the office and my Lord Woodrow [President Woodrow Wilson] hath sent me a commission in his Army, which I am glad to get, but heavy at heart to think of quitting my scrivening. Still, as some fellow hath said, 'Easy come, easy go.' "

After the war, summing up his military career, F.P.A. wrote, "I didn't fight and I didn't shoot; but general, how I did salute, and I was the toughest looking bird in uniform you ever saw."

Although when he left for military service he described himself as "heavy at heart to think of quitting my scrivening," he steadfastly professed to dislike writing. He once remarked dourly to an interviewer, "The only people who like to write terribly are those who do." Yet a better clue to his feelings lies in his resigned comment that, "Journalism's a shrew and a scold; I like her; she makes you sick, she makes you old; I like her."

In 1927, he and Harry Hansen compiled a book of questions and answers entitled "Answer This One," a volume that revealed F.P.A.'s lively interest in quizzes and questionnaires. A natural climax of this trend came in 1938, when Adams became a charter member of the "Information Please" radio panel. The "board of experts" on this program, including John Kiernan, Clifton Fadiman, and Oscar Levant, for several years answered an astonishing variety of questions and attracted thousands of faithful listeners.

Reviewing his radio and writing careers in later years, Adams remarked, "We went on the air with the 'Information Please' program first for peanuts, Clifton Fadiman, myself and the college professors. About all I made was railroad fare. Nobody would buy us." But by 1941, the program was paying him $900 a week. Not long after that, he reflected that it was "harder to write two original paragraphs than to work eight years" on "Information Please."

Yet the wit and knowledge revealed in his writings dazzled two generations of newspaper readers and his "Conning Tower" column was widely syndicated. One of the reasons for this lay in the broadness of its interests; F.P.A.'s comments ranged from light to incisive; it was impossible to guess what would engage his attention from one day to the next, for virtually everything did, at some time.

A Giants fan, his lament over a famed Chicago Cubs double-play combination probably will be remembered as long as baseball is played: "These are the saddest of possible words: / 'Tinker to Evers to Chance.' / Trio of Bear Cubs and fleeter than birds / 'Tinker to Evers to Chance.' / Ruthlessly picking our gonfalon bubble / Making a Giant hit into a double / Words that are heavy with nothing but trouble: / 'Tinker to Evers to Chance.' "

Although he was sensitive to the color that slang can bring to the language, he was impatient with its overuse in lieu of conversation. In the New York *World*, he once wrote: "To the dull and stupificient / I too numerously meet / Am I tolerant and patient? I am absolutely sweet! / Yet a faint and shallow furrow / Deepens in my tranquil brow / When a braying human burro / says 'And how!' "

Sometimes his observations dealt with deeper subjects, prompting Robert H. ("Bob") Davis to remark that "F.P.A. swings a rhythmic, wicked pen at the foibles of the day."

As an example, his thoughts "rekalsomined from the campaign [presidential] of 1912" led him to this conclusion: "Resources wasted in campaigns / In oratory dry and juiceless / The waste of energy and brains / Strikes me as useless."

Two of his comments in the column "This Little World,"

written in postwar 1946, illustrate his knack for combining the light touch and the serious message. A New Dealer from the beginning, he wrote, "My 1946 broadcast medal goes to General Dwight Eisenhower. To my notion, he is the only person since F.D.R. who makes the listener feel that he is being singled out, that the speaker is talking especially to him. It isn't technique or art, it is that the general probably likes people. To paraphrase 'Old Grimes,' who 'had no ruffles on his shirt,' of Eisenhower it may be said, 'He had no malice in his mind, no stuffing in his shirt.'"

In February of the same year, Adams wrote, paraphrasing a poem of the seventeenth-century English poet Robert Herrick: "Whenas in nylons, Julia goes / Then, then methinks, how fairly blows the liquefaction of her hose / But when the girls in line I see / To get a pair or two or three / O how that nonsense tickleth me."

The reference was to the fact that nylon stockings were in short supply immediately after World War II. He went on to say, "The long lines that used to form (during the war) to get cigarets looked as ridiculous to me as the nylon queues do . . . it all seems a little silly to anybody who has seen the long lines forming, hours before the *baekereien* and *fleischereien* opened in the cities and villages of Germany. Women were a mournful sight in Bavaria, clutching ration coupons to get the week's loaf of bread and a morsel of meat."

Mr. Adams' marriage to Minna Schwartz of Cheyenne, Wyoming, on November 15, 1904, ended in divorce, as did a second marriage, in 1925, to Esther Sayles Root, author and drama critic, who was the mother of his four children, Anthony, Timothy, Persephone, and Jonathan. The guest list of those attending his wedding to Miss Root not only indicates the professional stature he had attained; it also reveals the fact that he confined his friendships to the intelligentsia of the newspaper and literary world.

Reporters at the wedding, in Stamford, Connecticut, noted that those present included Edna St. Vincent Millay, Heywood Broun, Elinor Wylie, William Rose Benét, Deems Taylor, Mr. and Mrs. Bernard Baruch, Mr. and Mrs. Ring W. Lardner, Edna Ferber, Alexander Woollcott, Dorothy Parker, Harold Ross, guiding light of *The New Yorker*, Mr. and Mrs. Arthur Krock, and John Dos Passos.

Again, when F.P.A. left the New York *Post* in 1941, it was because, as *Time* magazine phrases it, "the Adams style of poetry à la Horace and Herrick was too fancy for the subway trade."

Adams once wrote, in a brief autobiography for the *Literary Digest* in 1934, "If I had enough money, I should do no work, but as long as I have to work, I would rather do what I do than anything else." He did produce a great deal. In addition to his widely read newspaper columns, he collaborated with O. Henry on a musical comedy, "Lo" (1909) and his books included *Tobogganing on Parnassus* (1910), *In Other Words* (1912), *By and Large* (1914), *Weights and Measures* (1917), *Something Else Again* (1920), *Overset* (1922), *So There!* (1922), *So Much Velvet* (1924), *Half a Loaf* (1927), *Christopher Columbus* (1931), *A Diary of Our Own Samuel Pepys* (1935), and *The Melancholy Lute* (1936).

In 1955, Adams entered a nursing home. He was often visited by such friends as John Kiernan, Clifton Fadiman, and Oscar Levant, but he did no more writing. He died on March 24, 1960, at the age of 78, at which time he was described in a United Press International article as "one of the all-time giants of American humor."

Long ago, Vice President Thomas Riley Marshall re-marked to John Crockett, Chief Clerk of the United States Senate, "What this country needs is a good five-cent cigar." In 1932, F.P.A. wrote, "What this country needs is a good five-cent nickel."

It was this kind of comment, so characteristic of Adams, that prompted a reviewer to write what might well serve as F.P.A.'s epitaph: "He shot folly without making a wry face."

> The rich man has his motor car
> His country and his town estate.
> He smokes a fifty-cent cigar
> And jeers at Fate.
>
> · · · · ·
>
> Yet though my lamp burn low and dim,
> Though I must slave for livelihood—
> Think you that I would change with him?
> You bet I would!
> —*The Rich Man*

RICHARD WILLARD ARMOUR

[1906–   ]

Richard armour's name has appeared in so many books and magazines in connection with so many pithy and witty capsule comments (in both verse and prose) about the cracks in life's cement that he is an old friend to thousands who have never met him. He is a true humorist.

That is to say, Richard Armour finds it possible (if not compulsive) to be candidly playful and irreverent about every aspect of what we are—and for that matter, what he himself is. For he does not leave himself out; in his light laughter, tempered with mercy, there is the assurance that he is not standing off saying, "What a strange lot you are," but rather that he stands before his bathroom mirror in the morning, relating himself spontaneously to the whole human lot, and concluding that "we are funny, you and I, in most of what we do, and it is a fortunate thing that we can recognize it."

Apart from the fact that he writes adroitly—the brevity of much of his humorous verse demands the precise word and the exact order of events—Armour's popularity stems from his obvious knowledge of subject and his empathy with his fellow men (including women and children), so often fumbling and frustrated by the daily doings of life.

18

He has no sacred cows. For example: He has written books. Books have jacket blurbs. Jacket blurbs tell what the books are about and help to sell them. The more books sold, the more money the author makes. Yet Richard Armour does not hesitate to hold up the jacket blurb to his lamp of truth and stick pins in it: "Consider please, the jacket blurb, / [that] hymns / The newborn masterpiece and limns / Its excellence, importance, justness, / Necessity, and downright mustness. . . ."

In 1963, referring to Armour's book entitled *The Medical Muse, or What to Do Until the Patient Comes,* Dr. Charles W. Mayo remarked: "Plato of Athens, who never was known to laugh very much in his youth, had a low opinion of poets. He thought that in the ideal republic, all poets should be banished from the realm. Had he been exposed to some of the soaring wit and fancy of a well-tempered artificer like Richard Armour, he might have improved both in disposition and some of his gloomier pronouncements."

The fact that such an eminent member of the medical profession was disposed to praise Armour's spoof of doctors and doctoring is significant and typical of his readers' reactions. In that volume, for instance, the author had pointed out, among many other things, that no one but druggists can read the handwriting of doctors, and the simple, irrefutable truth of this observation amuses doctors as much as, and perhaps even more than, it does people outside the medical world.

Richard Armour has made similar literary sallies into the worlds of the golfer, the academician, and the teen-ager; he has explored, exploited, and occasionally exploded history; he has re-examined, with tongue in cheek and jeweler's revealing eyeglass, Shakespeare, American literature, and the classics, with the deftness that can arise only from love and first-hand knowledge.

Born in San Pedro, California, on July 25, 1906—the very threshold of an age in which American readers would demand more laughter and less affectation than ever before—Richard Armour's educational background is a splendid refutation of the idea that (a) successful professors have to be out of touch with the world, and that (b) good light verse can be written "off the top of the head" by anybody who can think of "funny things" and a handful of words that rhyme. Actually, what Dr. Armour is, what he has accomplished intellectually, are awesome, even by the most serious standards of those who never in their lives wrote (or even read) a line of light verse.

For nearly forty years, Dr. Armour has been either a teacher or dean at seven colleges and universities; from 1945 to 1963, he was professor of English at Claremont Graduate School. He is presently Balch lecturer in English literature and dean of the faculty at Scripps College, Claremont, California.

The route by which he came to his present professional position is evidence of his characteristic energy and ability. A member of Phi Beta Kappa, Richard Armour was educated at Pomona College, Claremont, from which he received his bachelor's degree in 1927, and at Harvard University, where he earned his master's and bachelor's degrees, the latter in 1933.

Since then, he has been an instructor at the University of Texas (1928–29); Northwestern University (1930–31); professor of English and head of the division of modern languages, College of the Ozarks, (1932–33); American lecturer at the University of Freiberg, West Germany (1933–34); professor of English, Wells College (1934–35); Carnegie visiting professor, University of Hawaii (1957); and in 1931 he was Dexter Scholar (research fellow) from Harvard at the John Forster Library, Victoria and Albert Museum, in London.

As important as the scholarship underlying these experiences is the versatility they represent; thus, Dr. Armour has taught in small colleges, large universities, coeducational institutions, colleges for women, and a graduate school; he has also held research fellowships abroad (in both England and France) and has lectured at many colleges throughout the United States, with all the accompanying kaleidoscope of human experiences.

Thus, his laughter is that of a man of letters who was in fact serious before he was funny. His critical studies and biographies include *Barry Cornwall: A Biography of Bryan Waller Procter, The Literary Recollections of Barry Cornwall, Coleridge, the Talker* (written in collaboration with R. F. Howes), and a 3-act play, *To These Dark Steps* (written with Bown Adams), inspired by the life of John Milton.

Few sensitive persons of lesser learning would have been able to concoct such humorous works as Armour's *Twisted Tales from Shakespeare* or his *American Lit Relit*, for if, to employ another of his titles, a writer wishes to attempt *The Classics Reclassified*, he must first be on intimate terms with the classics themselves, as old and revered friends.

It is revealing that Armour's doctorate is in philology, the study that specifically concerns itself with the cultures of civilized peoples as revealed in their languages, literatures, and religions; the word itself, translated literally from the Greek, means "love of learning." In all of Armour's light verse (and in his equally light prose) there is repeated evidence of this love; it may be capricious or irreverent, but its depth and warmth are unmistakable. In speaking of his doctoral studies, he once remarked, rather wistfully, "I can still recite the Lord's Prayer in Gothic, but there aren't any Goths around to hear it."

The factor of energy that has made Armour an ambitious scholar and a prolific writer is astounding; coupled with a mind constantly in motion and the self-discipline that is essential to any serious creativity, it is a good object lesson to so many of us who excuse our lack of achievement by saying, "I just don't have time." As interviewer Sidney Fields noted in the Boston (Mass.) *Herald* in December, 1965, "In the past thirty years, Mr. Armour has written 29 books and 5,000 magazine pieces, all satire with a sting of truth behind the humor."

He himself has recalled that what "set him off" on a career of writing light verse was the fact that in 1937 he sold some couplets to the *Saturday Evening Post* and *The New Yorker*. Not long ago, he estimated that for the last twenty years, he has averaged three verses a day, and said that he tries to keep sixty verses in the mail at all times, en route to some of the more than one hundred magazines in the United States and England to which he contributes.

In his "spare time," Richard Armour married Kathleen Fauntleroy Stevens (in 1932); became the father of two children, Geoffrey Stevens and Karin Elizabeth, who have unquestionably inspired a share of his rhythmic meanderings; and acquired a shaggy dog, appropriately named "Happy."

What kinds of things strike him as being funny?

His favorite subject is women; next, is teen-agers. He finds that "women are endlessly fascinating, infinitely various and always baffling." As for teen-agers, he believes they both attract and repel. When his own children were teen-agers, he used them frequently as subjects, but never critically. "You wouldn't hit an invalid, would you?" he asked. "Adolescence is a disease, and there's no wonder drug for it. If another Dr. Salk comes along with a vaccine for adolescence, he'll get the Nobel Prize, but the question is—would it be for medicine or peace?"

It is Richard Armour, he alone, who has versified into American literature such homely truisms as these:

"It may be that an elephant never forgets because it has very little to remember."

"Little girls watch their fathers shave principally because they hope the latter will cut themselves."

"The awkward age of a child lasts from 1 to 20."

He has had many deep-reaching and delightful things to say about the academic world that has constituted such a large part of his life. These have included bright, crisp, and puckish treatment of roommates, the honor code, class attendance, grades, department heads, commencement speakers. Not the least perceptive of his observations appear in these typical Armour statements: "In ancient Athens, everyone knew Greek, and in ancient Rome, everyone knew Latin, even small children—which those who have taken elementary Greek or elementary Latin will find hard to believe.

"Universities wishing to teach a language which had little practical use but was good for mental discipline could have offered English, if they had thought of it."

Far more than a simple molder of epigrams, a creator of amusing jingles, Richard Armour's careers in verse and in education are inseparably linked by a thoughtful pleasure.

He once remarked, "It's a busy life," and that certainly would be considered an understatement by most who are far less busy than he. Its very busyness has placed him in a financial situation where he could stop teaching and live quite nicely on the royalties from his writing, but he says, "I love teaching too much. It seems that my whole life has been in colleges."

Yet light verse is his love as well; it is an intellectual gymnastics that he finds amusing and challenging; he is virtually a compulsive versifier now. As he explains it, "I just keep throwing my mind around. Sometimes I start with a cliché and twist it, and sometimes I start with a good last line and build up from there."

He has a fond feeling for his poems, a sort of paternal affection arising from the thought and pleasant effort he has expended on them. He knows, he says, "how they were worked up and worked over, better than I do the poems of anyone else. . . . I confess to a partiality for them, homely and ill-mannered as many of these verse children may be."

He thinks that male writers of light verse have done well, but that women "have done better. They seem to have a sharper eye, as well as a sharper pen."

Most critics of humor and satire in America would agree that Richard Armour—who once declared, "I do not care for public kisses / Or haughty looks or sneers or hisses / Or even poems such as this is / Unless they're mine."—also possesses an eye and mind of extraordinary sharpness.

> Now that I'm almost up the ladder
> I should, no doubt, be feeling gladder;
> It is quite fine, the view and such,
> If it just didn't shake so much.
> —*Ladder of Success*

MARGARET FISHBACK

[1904–   ]

In 1926, Margaret Fishback, daughter of a Washington lawyer, a native of the unruffled capital, and a graduate of Goucher College in Baltimore, arrived in New York, which was then considered a "fast and hard-boiled town."

Miss Fishback was jobless; she did not know what she was going to do, and her only effort in verse, composed in the fifth grade, had not betrayed her potential. It began, "I am an English sparrow and I live way up in a tree. . . ."

She was stagestruck; in retrospect, however, she said she did not think this was a handicap, because "it is so often the lever that propels girls into the metropolis, girls who afterward make their mark." In her case, ballet lessons enabled her to appear on the Metropolitan Opera stage six times as a "super" (supernumerary) in the ballet, for which she was paid one dollar a performance.

Obviously, ballet was not remunerative. Accordingly, when her roommate in a girls' club told her of an opening in a large "publicity" firm—although she was slightly vague as to what constituted public relations—she walked into the office and demanded an interview with the president. A few days later, she really got the interview; on the following Monday she started work. "Luck, pure and simple," Miss Fishback remarked later.

Her first assignment was to make a speech before a group of women whom she was supposed to organize for a fundraising drive, and she described herself as "scared to death." Once described as the world's worst typist, she nevertheless pecked out letters to the wealthy (obviously with certain success, since she retained her job with the firm), urging them to forward a check for a worthy charity.

Destiny works in strange ways. Out for lunch on a sunny day in late March, Miss Fishback passed a pushcart full of potted plants. When she got back to the office, she typed out: "How do I know that winter relents? / Arbutus is down to seventy cents."

Franklin P. Adams, then conducting his "Conning Tower" column in the New York *World*, published the couplet, and this was the beginning of Margaret Fishback's outstanding career in light verse writing. She immediately wrote more and sold one of them to *The New Yorker* magazine, thus bypassing at one stroke the initial period of rejection slips and heartbreak that every poet is supposed to experience. After three years of writing verse, an encouraging amount of which was published, she inclined toward a writing career and searched for a livelier job that would allow her to do some.

When the advertising department of Macy's in New York hired her as an assistant copy writer at $40 a week, it initiated a revolution of sorts that neither the store management nor Margaret Fishback had anticipated. As a contemporary wrote, "Until the Fishback girl arrived, Macy's ads had been solemnly conventional. After a brief apprenticeship, she began inserting flippant rhymes and wisecracks. She even insulted the merchandise."

Once, for example, she discovered a two-foot cake tester in the kitchen utensils department. She decided this was a ridiculous length and wrote an ad saying, "This cake tester will come in handy the next time you bake a cake two feet high."

The management undoubtedly shuddered. But orders for the cake tester came pouring in. There were 2,200 mail orders, 1,700 telephone orders, and a total of 19,000 sales. There were even orders from Alaska. Macy's had only a few hundred testers in stock, at six cents each. The store had to have thousands specially made up, at much more than the sales price, but a valuable lesson had been learned, that humor can sell more goods than seriousness. Margaret Fishback had started a trend, and other major companies soon copied her light approach to salesmanship.

In 1931, interviewer Geraldine Sartain found Miss Fishback to be " a slim, yellow-haired girl in a softly clinging yellow dress, one of the highest-paid advertising women in America in a walnut-paneled office thirteen floors above West 35th Street, and completely free of vanity or self-consciousness."

" 'Now this is what I mean when I speak of humor in advertising', said Miss Fishback. She picked up a newspaper clipping topped with an amusing sketch of a deer that had eight antlers, with a hat perched on each. The Fishback verse accompanying the illustration read: 'The reindeer finds Manhattan heat / A shattering experience / For once he ventures on the street / He undergoes the great expense / Of weighting eight straw hats upon / His antlers, in the hope that they / Will separate him from the sun / And keep him cool despite the day. / Poor deer, his overhead is quite / Absurd.

He should be told to go / To Macy's, where the Fahrenheit / Is like the prices, sweet and low.' "

During this period, at odd moments, Margaret Fishback was dashing off (she made it seem as easy as this, whether or not it was) poems for such publications as *Vanity Fair*, *The New Yorker* and the *Saturday Evening Post*. Her poetry lightly lampooned human foibles; it flowed with easy grace, and although sharp and satiric nevertheless reflected not only her extraordinary articulateness, but her zest for life and work. She still attributed her success to "grand luck," a most modest appraisal, but admitted that she thought imagination, an excellent vocabulary, a sense of rhythm in writing, and a controlled sense of humor were invaluable to anyone who wanted to write light verse.

Miss Fishback made an interesting comment on humor in 1931, differentiating between her belief in it and its necessity. She remarked, "Most of the successful persons in the world are not blessed with humor to a great degree. Therefore, I don't think of it as essential to success. Rather do I consider it an absolute essential in one's personal life, in making for personal happiness."

By the early thirties, her published volumes of verse were attracting first-rate critical attention. Of *I Feel Better Now* (1932), poet William Rose Benét wrote, "Miss Fishback deserves to be admitted to the small fraternity of good light verse writers," and of *Out of My Head* (1933), Mr. Benét added, "Nimble is the right word for her verses . . . her trifles are not tremendous, but neither are they altogether trivial."

But the interesting thing about Margaret Fishback is that there have been two Margaret Fishbacks, poetically speaking, as reflected in the subject matter and philosophy of her published verse, and the mid-thirties reveal this transition most startlingly.

In the first era of her creativity, she was the lighthearted sophisticate, the bachelor girl in the big city, who cared not for cooking or children, and who wrote of romance casually. Still, there were hints even then that Miss Fishback was a woman of deeper feeling than she chose to reveal in her rhymings. At one point, wondering frustratedly why she was equipped with a conscience, she wrote, "Is Cotton Mather in my blood / That I should rigidly eschew / The pleasure I'm entitled to?" Change, when it came, was drastic.

Interviewer Charles D. Rice wrote, "Abruptly in 1935, contemporaries described her [advertising] copy as dull, syrupy and running to rugs. It was discovered that she had fallen in love with Alberto G. Antolini, the company's rug buyer, and they were married. She promptly reversed all her previous pledges about refusing to commute, even for love, and they bought a house in New Jersey, a long and cruel trip twice a day. Eventually, they purchased a farmhouse in Maine with a well that went down 172 feet before they found water. It is reported that she "not only learned to cook, but to shingle a roof."

By 1939, her hair was a "warm shade of reddish blond, done simply with two swept-up curls like small wings on either side of her forehead and large, expressive light eyes." Within, she had been transformed from the free, self-reliant woman of *I Feel Better Now* to an off-handed sentimentalist, as portrayed in her book of verses, *I Take It Back*.

In her spare time, she was writing a 60,000-word book on etiquette, at the request of her publishers. "Verses, you can dash off at lunch," she remarked, "but this sounds like a big job to me." (It took her four months to write, which is a very creditable pace.)

As a result of this new chore, she found that "people ask me all kinds of questions that tax my common sense."

For example, there was the young man who found it necessary to attend a party announcing his engagement. He felt uneasy about what he should say, and asked Margaret Fishback for a formula. "I told him about all he could do was to stand around and look foolish," she recalled, but this was the flippant Miss Fishback of Era No. 1 speaking, and by the time she got home from the office, she had a guilty feeling that she had failed a member of her public. So, the sentimental Miss Fishback of Era No. 2 phoned the young man, and read to him the advice of an older etiquette authority for the guidance of persons in an engaged predicament.

As a married working woman, she had definite ideas about business and social conduct. She advised, "Use common sense, tempered with lots of imagination and understanding of the boss. In general, of course, all unnecessary interruptions are out of place in an office. This goes for relatives and friends who drop in at odd hours.

"Underlings should register respect, whether it is merited or not, because business demands that people be good soldiers. That's etiquette. Insubordination isn't cricket.

"Women in business should be neither melodramatic nor aggressively feminine. It is neither sporting nor well-bred to trade on sex in the office.

"Executives can squeeze more work out of their employes with less effort if they follow simple rules and instincts of decent civil conduct. To be polite and pleasant takes no more time. Human beings can accomplish the impossible when they are stimulated by a reasonable amount of applause.

"People who marry and keep on working should be in the

same business and preferably in the same firm [as she and her husband were], because it promotes understanding of each other's problems.

"As for social life, small dinners are most successful. Late evening parties and supper after the theater are the bane of working people's existence. I believe in expedient entertaining."

In 1941, she entered a third era, which some have called the "Little Tony Period," and in which the emphasis on domesticity was intensified. A contemporary reported, "Margaret was going to have a baby. It was a closely guarded secret among her 2,000 most intimate friends. The girl who hated brats suddenly became a changed person. When she left Macy's of an evening, she often astonished the Seventh Avenue street urchins by patting them on the head.

"She kept on with her job until the very last and left in a flood of good wishes. She emerged from the ether and started writing poems about every new development in her son's life. She also indulged in part-time writing for Macy's and other chores."

Professional reaction to her book of verses *Look Who's a Mother* (1945) clearly encouraged her to write "about every new development in her son's life." One reviewer commented, "What gives her book its lift above pediatrics is that most of it is given to brief, pointed typically Fishbackian verses in which babies are, among other things, firmly and affectionately debunked." Another critic wrote, "This is a good thing. Real mothers know that pretty as a baby may be, all bundled up in swansdown or in gush, the less he has on, the more entrancing he will be."

By 1948, "blond, energetic and a merry-go-round of cheerful confusion," Margaret Fishback had, strictly as a sideline, sold approximately 5,000 humorous poems to virtually every magazine printed in English, in addition to writing her eminently successful books of verses.

Poems Made Up to Take Out (1948) was the title of one of her volumes of verse and, with certain significance, this motto was transferred to her personal stationery. For Miss Fishback's professional career, both in business and verse, has been exemplary for the manner in which she disciplines her seemingly boundless energies. Because she is efficient, she has been able to be wife, mother, business woman, poet, hostess, P-TA member, and keeper of the hearth without dropping an iambic, or missing a deadline.

Just as her vigor for life is unusual, so is the versatility of her interest, as reflected by the range of subjects about which she has written verses. She has been inspired to rhyme by subways and offices, cats and dogs, supermarkets and rainbows; by Santa Claus, the mysteries of spelling ("a cup of coughey . . . might do me gould"), and by fall-out shelters (she concluded that they cost too much and that she could calm her nerves otherwise.) Her pen has been moved to record the truism that speeding ambulances pick up one patient and knock down two more; to deplore the fact that she has a frank and open face rather than "an enigmatic smile and heavy-lidded eyes," siren-style, and to comment on the view from a Maine bath tub ("a pine . . . quite divine)."

The publication *Printer's Ink* in October, 1959, noted that Miss Fishback had joined the copy department of a New York advertising agency, commenting, "Her work as copy chief in the 1930s and early '40s for Macy's was an important contribution to what is regarded as a golden age of department store advertising. Much of her institutional advertising for Macy's was humorous.

"She has published seven books and has contributed verse and prose to *Good Housekeeping, Ladies' Home Journal, Look, McCall's, The New Yorker* and *Saturday Evening Post.* She left Macy's in 1942 to devote more time to her family. Now, with her son in college, she can plunge back full time; she has done magazine and book writing, and part-time advertising writing in the interim, and now has a good chance to use her skills as a creative humorist."

In 1963, in his column "In and Out of Books," Lewis Nichols of *The New York Times* took notice of what has happened professionally, not only to Margaret Fishback, but to all American writers of light verse. Nichols wrote: "Poets have a rough time these days, and of all poets, those who write light verse may have the roughest. Ogden Nash, who probably could be called the dean of this trade, has said so. Margaret Fishback, who probably could be called the dean of women, echoed this the other day. [She said], 'Magazines have vanished; other outlets have dried up; you can't make a living from verse alone.' "

Thus it was that Margaret Fishback, a professional writer of verse since 1927, went from 1946 for almost fifteen years before publishing her eighth book, *Poems Made Up to Take Out,* principally because, in her words, "The big question for all of us these days is how to go about selling our stuff." Characteristically, however, she wrote during all this time.

Nichols concluded, "*Poems Made Up to Take Out* still holds as a business enterprise. But the customers aren't knocking on the door the way they did. Dean Nash has said so. Dean Fishback agrees. Light verse is a form of humor and if you look around carefully, you may—you just may—be able to name five humorists who still are working. Humor's disappearing."

The view from here is quite divine
A nicer tub I never knew
Outside the window, there's a pine
The view from here is quite divine
An etching that I wish were mine
So sweet it is against the blue
The view from here is quite divine
A nicer tub I never knew.
—*Triolet in a Maine Bathtub*

ARTHUR GUITERMAN

[1871-1943]

IF THERE IS a father of American light verse, Arthur Guiterman, far more scholar than mere jester and a writer who for many years made an excellent living in this field, is well qualified for the title. Of his ability to derive an ample income solely from the production of light verse, he once wrote to a guest, "Your lunch, by the way, including the salad, was part of a ballad / We live on a stanza a day."

But to suggest that Arthur Guiterman was simply a rhymster who made jingles pay is to ignore the many facets of achievement that mark him as an outstanding literary figure.

He was born in Vienna in 1876, while his parents were there on business, and because of the anxiety of his mother, a native of Ohio, that there should be no possible doubt of his citizenship, his name was registered at the American Embassy within twenty-four hours of his birth. In his third year, the family returned to New York and after public schools, he was educated at the College of the City of New York, from which he was graduated in 1891. His college record offered a major clue as to what kind of man he was to become.

Although when he was five, he had to wear steel braces on both ankles and was so weak that he went upstairs on all fours, while at college he was active in lacrosse, tennis, and rowing; was captain of the bicycle club; and, as the best sprinter of his year, was a member of the college track team in the inter-collegiate games of 1891.

At the same time, he received the Ward medal for the highest rating in English composition and was elected to Phi Beta Kappa. This combination of erudition, physical fitness, and love of the outdoors were fundamental characteristics of Arthur Guiterman throughout his life.

His first verses, written at the age of eight, were about butterflies; a lover of animals, his childhood ambition was to be a naturalist. In later years, interviewers described him as "a powerful tennis player, despite his glasses, an enthusiastic canoeist and hiker," and he once went on a walking tour through the Pryrenees with his wife, the former Vida Lindo, whom he married in 1909.

It once was written of Arthur Guiterman, who adopted the practice of living in a New York apartment in winter and in Maine in summer, that "contrary to popular custom, he does not make unpleasant remarks about women, probably because he has lived in conspicuous marital felicity for twenty years." As "Vida," Mrs. Guiterman was the subject of and inspiration for many of his poems.

Some early verses that brought him widespread fame also puzzled Guiterman; he could not understand why they caused such furor, for, as he pointed out, "I have written cleverer verses." (It is characteristic of Guiterman that he never referred to his writings as poems, even though he became president of the Poetry Society of America and Joyce Kilmer once called him "the most American of poets.")

The four quatrains to which he referred were titled "Strictly Germ-Proof" and concern the adventures of an "antiseptic baby" and a "prophylactic pup." The child and the dog steamed, sterilized, and fumigated a rabbit so they could play with it in an atmosphere of which Guiterman wrote: "There's not a micrococcus in the garden where they play."

He sent the quatrains to *The New York Times* and not having heard from the newspaper, also submitted them to the editors of *Woman's Home Companion,* for which he was also writing. The *Times,* he discovered, already had the verses set in type, but allowed the magazine to publish them and surrendered its rights.

For thirteen years, these lines were stolen and read around the world; they were plagiarized at least six times, and translated, among other languages, into Esperanto. The ramifications of this literary drama of stealing, accusations, and forged affidavits extended to London, South Africa, and Australia, and one man sold "Strictly Germ-Proof" to a New York newspaper two years after it first appeared in the Woman's Home Companion.

Arthur Guiterman was the originator of the popular (and much imitated) rhymed book reviews that appeared under his by-line each week in the original *Life* magazine. One of the most famous of these is the delightful summary of *Bella Donna,* the story of a poisonous female created by Robert Hichens, who fed her husband powdered lead and then, when her infamy was exposed, fled across the Egyptian sands to a lover who, she then discovered, had changed his mind about wanting her.

Of this upsetting chain of events, Guiterman wrote: "He cast her off. In blinded haste / Before the birds began to twitter / She staggered far across the waste. / I hope to God a lion bit her!"

Of another book, he rhymed: "Here is a romance by Mrs.

Glyn / Full of tabasco and dynamite / Heroine draped in a leopard skin / Captures the heart of an anchorite."

And some contained small barbs, such as his comment on Temple Bailey's *The Tin Soldier:* "A tale of strife that bids one think / Of roses, ribbons, blushes, kisses / Oh would that I could write as pink / And popular a work as this is."

In the meantime, he had contributed verses to a New York newspaper without pay for eight years before he realized they had a monetary value. For example, one can find in F.P.A.'s "Conning Tower" one of these early Guitermans: "He traveled fast / He traveled far / He sought at vesper time / A spot where one might park a car / And yet commit no crime."

As his professional stature grew, Arthur Guiterman became something of a legend. He was a warm and profound philosopher ("I want my hills / The trail that scorns the hollow / Up, up the ragged shale / Where few will follow.") He was a fine scholar, once described by Mary Day Winn in the New York *Herald-Tribune* as "well-read, far traveled . . . a conscientious craftsman who puts his best effort into even the least thing he does; who probably knows more about and has more skill with poetic forms than any other American poet and who hates 'vers libre,' which he describes as 'prose set in gasps.' "

By nature a destroyer of pretense, a critic of poets who act like poets, a retiring fellow who at regular intervals shut himself in his study and, to use his own phrase, "sweat blood" producing witty, lighthearted lyrics, he did not lunch at the Algonquin Hotel "with that little group of serious boosters, oraculating on art and men and love and each other." The reference was to the "Round Table," a group of his contemporaries, several writing regularly for *The New Yorker.*

Yet Guiterman by no means ignored those writers strug-
gling to emulate his success. For the guidance of the poet
who "would eke out his existence at verse," he drew up certain specific commandments, including the following:

"Don't think of yourself as a poet, and don't dress the
part; don't call your quarters a garret or studio; don't com-
plain of lack of appreciation. In the long run, no really good
work can escape appreciation.

"Don't think you are entitled to special rights, privileges
and immunity because you are a literary person, or have any
more reason to consider your possible lack of fame a griev-
ance against the world than has any shipping clerk or traveling salesman.

"Don't use e'er for ever or o'er for over, and don't say did
go for went, even if you need an extra syllable.

"Don't have your book published at your own expense.

"Don't write hymns to the Great God Pan. He is dead.
Let him rest in peace."

As these "commandments" suggest, he was an unusual
combination of serious humorist and practical poet. An interviewer in the twenties found him to be "a man of medium
size, possessing a forehead slightly reminiscent of William
Jennings Bryan, kindly, humorous brown eyes, and a high-
pitched, though pleasant voice and a precise manner of speaking," and the interview produced a revealing anecdote.

Guiterman was serving on a jury, made up, as he recalled
it, of "a poet, an actor and ten hard-headed businessmen." A
pretty, weeping girl was suing a corporation for large damages. The ten businessmen, Guiterman related, wanted to
give her the damages "even though the claim was fradulent
on the face of it." The poet (Guiterman), supported by the
actor, held out for what usually is regarded as unpoetical and

untheatrical clear-headedness and finally won the remainder of the jury to the pro-Guiterman side.

He was not afraid, as many writers are, of being under-valued if he indulged in humor. As to this, Guiterman commented, "It is unfortunate that the natural versatility of the human mind is not sufficiently recognized and that labeling and pigeon-holing persist . . . although I, personally, am not obsessed by it."

As an example of his successful ventures into serious writing, despite the fact that his major reputation was built on light verse, in collaboration with Lawrence Langner, he prepared an adaptation of Molière's *L'École des Maris* in English rhymed verse which, as *The School for Husbands*, was produced successfully by the Theater Guild in 1933. Guiterman also wrote the libretto and lyrics for the opera *The Man Without a Country*, with a score by Walter Damrosch, which was produced by the Metropolitan Opera Company during the 1937–38 season.

He also produced seventeen books between 1907 and 1939, including *Ballads of Old New York* (1920), *The Light Guitar* (1923), *Death of General Putnam and 101 Other Poems* (1935), and *Gaily the Troubadour* (1936).

It was Guiterman's opinion that "being a poet of any sort is a serious business. There is no such thing as poetic license. The poet has a definite duty to his native tongue, and this applies, not only to the correct use of words, but also to the showing of proper respect to them by assuring their correct pronunciation. If he does not do this, he is not playing the game."

The scholar's curiosity and perpetual appetite for words were hallmarks of Arthur Guiterman's professional identity. There once was an evening meeting of the Poetry Society of

America in New York, at which Lord Dunsany, Irish poet and dramatist, and John Drinkwater, English poet and dramatist, were guests of honor. Each, according to schedule, read from his published works. Then, as the subsequent discussion opened, the two speakers fell upon what apparently was a pet bone of contention.

It was a friendly dispute, but nevertheless both spirited and serious, concerning the respective merits of rhymed verse and rhythmical prose. Each argued his point with conviction, and finally Lord Dunsany, with an air of propounding an absolutely unanswerable question, demanded: "Supposing you had a line of rhymed verse ending with the word 'wasp,' where, I ask you, could you find a rhyme for wasp?"

In the words of the Boston *Transcript's* Alice Lawton, "That was the evening's Parthian shot. Mr. Drinkwater produced no rhyme for 'wasp.' "

Arthur Guiterman was present. He later recalled, "You can find a rhyme for wasp. There is a perfectly good one in the dictionary. I found it at home that night. It is knosp and means a flower bud, or a budlike architectural ornament. Of course, having found it, I had to use it at once." (It is contained in "Kindness to Insects," included in the collection *The Light Guitar*.)

In January, 1940, reviewing his volume entitled *Lyric Laughter*, *Time* magazine acknowledged Arthur Guiterman as "probably the best professional writer of light verse in the United States today," and went on to say that "for the past 43 years, his verselets have kept winking at readers from odd corners of magazines and newspapers and from the formal pages of 14 books. . . .

"[He is] a sweetmeat maker, who knows how words can be tenderized, much like prunes, to please the palates of the literarily refined. . . . Moralistic puzzles . . . are stock grist for Mr. Guiterman's mill . . . his jingles do something effective about things which it is conventionally taken for granted that nothing can be done about. He writes almost exclusively to offer reassurance and sometimes succeeds in conveying it, in a world in which 'romans' rhymes with 'abdomens.' "

On January 11, 1943, Arthur Guiterman died, at the age of 76, in Pittsburgh. His death came late in the evening after a sudden collapse that morning at nearby Oakland, where he was scheduled to make a lecture appearance.

He will be recalled by many for his insistence upon intellectual honesty and as the writer who once said: "I have often noticed at the Poetry Society that, after a poem has been read and applauded, when someone dares to get up and inquire what it means, there is likely to be a great outcry to the effect that one cannot analyze a beautiful thing. That is a basic absurdity and represents nothing but a variety of snobbery.

"Some will declare indignantly, 'This thought is too great to be definitely expressed. There is truth, I am certain, in the lines 'whatever deep or shallow, new or old / is clearly thought, can be as clearly told.' The writer who does not say what he has to say clearly, is shirking his job."

Some mispronounced Guiterman's name. An editorial friend, appealed to for the correct pronunciation, replied in the following couplet: "There ain't no better, fitter man / Than Mr. Arthur Guiterman."

The many thousands who read his prolific outpouring of verse over the decades, and the several writers who are, by their own admission, indebted to his advice and example, undoubtedly would agree with this appraisal.

ARTHUR GUITERMAN

The Antiseptic Baby and the Prophylactic Pup
Were playing in the garden when the Bunny gamboled up;
They looked upon the Creature with a loathing undisguised;—
It wasn't Disinfected and it wasn't Sterilized.

—Strictly Germ-Proof

OLIVER HERFORD

[1863-1935]

THAT VERY delightful wit and artist," President Woodrow Wilson once remarked in referring to Oliver Herford, and many thousands would have seconded the President's evaluation of this extraordinary poet and playwright. If there was one quality of Oliver Herford that was outstanding among his many talents, it would have to be the facility with which he caused the English language to do his precise bidding.

From 1893 to 1931, Oliver Herford probably wrote at least fifty books of what has been described as "artistic nonsense," illustrated four of them, and had four plays produced. With regard to the total number of books, it is necessary to say "probably," because, although lesser men would have known exactly, he was not sure himself how many he had written, and could not even remember the titles of some.

At the turn of the century, Herford's ready tongue, as well as his facile pen, had gained for him an international reputation; many of the comments that graced his brilliant conversation were repeated or appropriated by the less gifted. William Dean Howells, an eminent novelist in his own right and at one time editor-in-chief of *The Atlantic*

Monthly, described Oliver Herford as "the Charles Lamb of his day." The reference was undoubtedly to that period in the life of Charles Lamb, the nineteenth-century English essayist and critic, when he surrounded himself with a circle of literary friends during weekly or monthly "at homes" and gained widespread fame as both a conversationalist and an inspirer of conversation.

One of Herford's most quoted remarks concerned his wife. He remarked to a friend one day that he had to do an errand, adding that it was just one of his wife's whims.

"Then why do it?" asked the friend.

"You don't know Margaret," Herford replied with a sigh. "She has a whim of iron."

This talented writer of light verse (and much else) was born in Sheffield, England, the son of a Unitarian clergyman, the Reverend Dr. Brooke Herford, who was an author of religious works. When Oliver was six, the family moved to the United States, where his father held pastorates in Boston and Chicago. Oliver was educated at Lancaster College in England, at Antioch College, Yellow Springs, Ohio. In addition, he studied art at the Slade School in London and at Julien's in Paris.

His work, speech, and dress (he wore a high stiff collar and sported a monocle in the English fashion) reflected this cosmopolitan background. Soon after completing his studies, he began contributing to humorous magazines, through which he probably reached his largest audience. Children became acquainted with him in the pages of *St. Nicholas*, then a widely read juvenile publication, and grew up to enjoy him even more in the *Century, Harper's*, and *Ladies' Home Journal* magazines.

When Norman Hapgood, editor and author, was in charge

of *Harper's Weekly* (1913–16), Herford's "Pen and Inklings" (the title of his first book, published in 1893) department was a noteworthy feature of the publication. The versatile humorist's astonishing cartoon cover on that magazine, depicting the Grand Boss of New York City's powerful political club, the Tammany Society, posed shiveringly as "September Morn" has been called one of the most powerful of its kind since the work of the great political cartoonist Thomas Nast. "September Morn," an early twentieth-century painting by the French artist Paul Chabas, depicts a young woman standing nude in what appears to be uncomfortably cool water. Herford's version was published under the appropriate title "November Morn," since it appeared just after a severe Tammany defeat at the polls.

In 1903, the American actor Edward Hugh Sothern and his wife, Virginia Harned, an actress in her own right, gave a dinner party; their guests included Margaret Regan, who came from Manchester, England, and Oliver Herford. Miss Regan had come to the United States to play a minor role in a Daniel Frohman play starring Cecilia ("Cissie") Loftus, with whom she had attended convent school.

Both Miss Regan and Mr. Herford were persons of exceptional charm and ability; each was an excellent conversationalist and each could write and draw. She was, by all standards, a beautiful woman; she also possessed the master of arts and doctor of science degrees, and wrote exquisitely polished light humorous verse. Miss Regan and Mr. Herford, according to a contemporary account, "dominated" the dinner and very probably no one who knew them was surprised when they were married in the following year.

An account in the *American Journal Examiner* of September 9, 1906, reported that "they were married at the Hotel Breslin in New York and kept house in a charming little flat at the Criterion, No. 60 West 10th Street, and Mr. Herford had a studio at No. 83 Washington Place." It is characteristic that the studio possessed a cat named Boffin, for this was the man of whom the writer Carolyn Wells said, "No one is more successful than he in personifying animals." Many of Mr. Herford's works reveal his compassionate interest in creatures other than man.

Shortly after their marriage, the couple, walking along a New York street, met an acquaintance of Mr. Herford. The friend remarked, "I hear you are a benedict, Oliver." Herford, bowing to the lady at his side, replied, "Yes, and this my benedictine."

It was Mrs. Herford who conceived the idea of a weekly called *Dreamland*, which was published at Coney Island. A fundamental editorial rule of this enterprise was that no contribution could be accepted unless accompanied by proof that it had been rejected by at least three of the leading publishing houses.

The magazine contained such Herfordian gems as this: "The sloth enjoys a life of ease / He hangs inverted from the trees / And views life upside down / If you, my child, are nothing loath / To live in indolence and sloth / Unheeding the world's frown / You, too, unvexed by toil and strife / May take a humorous view of life."

Also, this philosophical quatrain: "Oh, yes, the wolf is bad, it's true / But how without him could you do? / If there were not a wolf, what good / Would be the tale of Riding Hood?"

Herford's humor knew no bounds or barriers; he found it wherever he looked. His volume entitled *The Bashful Earthquake and Other Verses and Fables*, which appeared in 1898,

47

was dedicated "To the illustrator, in grateful acknowledgment of his amiable condescension in lending his exquisitely delicate art to the embellishment of these poor verses, from his sincerest admirer, the author."

The illustrator and author were of course the same— Oliver Herford.

His delightfully droll *A Child's Primer of Natural History* (1899) was followed by *More Animals* (1901), which established his reputation; both books were instantly popular for their sparkling fooleries and sage philosophy disguised as lilting nonsense. An even more notable success was his inquiry into the nature of the universe "from a furry point of view," entitled *Rubaiyat of a Persian Kitten* (1904), copies of which were sold even in China.

By 1906, Herford, who has been called "the most quoted man in America," had created *A Little Book of Bores*, a catalogue of easily recognizable though less easily avoided social encumbrances, including: "E is the Egotist Dread / Who, as someone has wittily said / Will talk till he's blue / About himself when you / Want to talk about yourself instead." Unquestionably, Herford, by virtue of his own brilliance of speech, would have found bores—particularly conversational bores—intolerable.

Once he had established himself as a humorist, principally through contributions to magazines, Herford branched out into poetry and playwriting. It is interesting that he won his first literary successes at about the same time that his famous sister Beatrice (Mrs. Sidney W. Hayward) made her stage debut as a monologist. Herford illustrated her book *Monologues* in 1908, but, unlike his sister, could not be induced to mount a lecture platform or stage; nor could he be cajoled into delivering an after-dinner speech. His bons mots and

48

"Herfordisms" occurred only in the informal give-and-take of conversation, and often at the Players in New York, where he spent many congenial hours.

Critics and intimates (several of whom were also worthy wordsmiths, since this was something of a Golden Age for the art of gentle and genteel conversation) described him variously as "a whimsical genius who ignores all the rules for genius," the "virtuoso of the unexpected reply," and "the Peck's bad boy of Parnassus," a reference to the mountain in Greece that in ancient times was sacred to Apollo and the Muses, including the goddess of poetry.

Professionally, the quality, quantity, and versatility of his effort astounded even Times Square, urbane as it then was. At one time, Herford had a comedy and a musical show running in theaters next door to each other on 42nd Street. Enormously popular at the time was his series of "Cynic's Calendars," which he created with the author, Ethel Watts Mumford. In these, pert animals glistened with such gems of revised wisdom as "Actresses happen in the best of regulated families" and "A thing of duty is annoy forever." Yet at the opposite end of the intellectual scale, this was the same man who in 1908 produced *The Devil*, thus establishing himself as the first playwright to adapt a work of Ferenc Molnár for the American stage.

The kind of humor that appealed in that period indicates a great deal about those who found it amusing, for this was a far simpler and less sophisticated America. For example, in *Cupid's Almanac and Guide to Hearticulture*, which Herford produced with John Cecil Clay ("Dedicated to lovers and lovers of lovers"), an illustration of a commuter with harassed expression and arms full of bundles is titled "Commutation or Bundle-Bearer Weed." It is defined as "a sort of

49

combination between the hayseedia and the storeclothesia
. . . to be found all along the railroads. Very plentiful about
New York. Seems to flourish wonderfully in little hot houses."

The *Century* magazine of July 7, 1916, published his
verses addressed "To a Flea": "Who knows but through
your microscopic veins / Once flowed the blood of king or
pontiff grand? / Who knows what mighty chiefs your kin-
ship share? / Of one great Roman surely there remains / A
trace, else why, when falls the vengeful hand / Like Fabius,
are you always otherwhere?"

Oliver Herford was many things to many people—
charming poet, whimsical philosopher, trenchant cartoonist,
tenderly humorous interpreter of animals, provocative dramatist; at the same time, he was characterized by some as un-
conventional, irreverent, and irresponsible genius, prankish
artist, bohemian, droll eccentric, and even, in the words of a
contemporary reviewer, as a "sly recluse known to everyone
for his delicious volumes."

His interests and comments were focused virtually everywhere.

The old Life magazine published his poem commemorating
the Atlantic flight of Charles A. Lindbergh in 1927, a stirring
tribute, beginning "Arms and the boy I sing," which was
soon set to music and sung on radio broadcasts.

When a former President of the United States, Theodore
Roosevelt, went to Africa to hunt lions, Herford made it
very plain that his sympathies were with the lions.

It was also he who said of the New York Public Library
that it was there that one "learned the meaning of the expression 'reading between the lions,'" a pun inspired by the stone
figures of the king of beasts that recline at either side of steps
leading to the library's main entrance.

And it was he who wrote, in a "telephone girl's" (1930 idiom for switchboard operator) prayer, "O Lord, . . . for all wrong numbers I have gave and gave and gave . . . excuse it please."

Herford had absolutely no patience with pessimism; he called gloom for gloom's sake a pernicious form of self indulgence. He liked to have Mrs. Herford read aloud to him, but would not stand for morbid, depressing passages or unhappy endings; if she discovered that this was the case, she would improvise as she read, making the lot of the characters a more happy one.

His favorite refreshment of the day was afternoon tea. On one such occasion, someone insisted on reading the work of a young intellectual who wrote in what was described as "an acutely depressing way."

"I won't allow it," said Herford, jumping up. "None of us would be affected by it, but the servant girl might come into the room and hear you. Think what that would mean. She'd get the contagion and take to writing poems like that. Only they'd be better ones."

His "droll eccentricities" included riding escalators. He enjoyed this very much and would go blocks out of his way to indulge in this pastime. When he worked for *Life*, he would explain carefully to the passing bootblack that he only had time to have one shoe shined. He also told friends often that he had thought of working at home as he had done in earlier years, but didn't, realizing that it would entail cleaning out his desk.

That Herford had some difficulties with orderliness was also revealed in an interview in 1927 by Lawton Mackall of the New York *Herald-Tribune*, who wrote: "Even colored slips of paper that read 'Pay to the order of Oliver Herford' disappear into oblivion unless rescued by Mrs. Herford. But the greeting cards he receives at Christmas are carefully kept and opened for the first time on some hot day in July. He remarked, 'When other people's friends have gone away for the summer and neglect them, it certainly is gratifying and exciting to be cheerily greeted by everyone you know.'"

When Oliver Herford was 64, able to look back upon a life characterized by pleasant experiences, congenial associates, and professional success, interviewer Mackall noted that "he has dwelt in the same apartment near Gramercy Park in New York for more than 20 years [he lived there until his death eight years later] with the same wife. . . . He has a fresher outlook on life than Jackie Coogan [then 12 years old and a popular film star]; Mr. Herford is the wonder child who grew cleverer and cleverer."

Forty years later, this appraisal still holds; it is a delight to consider Oliver Herford and his achievements, for he was an outstanding product of a wonderfully peaceful age in which, oftener than now seems possible, a delicately turned phrase was one of the day's most important experiences.

> The Gargoyle often makes his perch
> On a cathedral or a church
> Where, mid ecclesiastic style,
> He smiles an early-Gothic smile.
> —*The Gargoyle*

SAMUEL GOODMAN
HOFFENSTEIN

[1890–1947]

Samuel hoffenstein died relatively young, in his 57th
year, and in the field of light verse, he is remembered principally for one volume; yet some of America's foremost
writers in this vein, including Ogden Nash, acknowledge
their literary indebtedness to him. Essentially this is so because Hoffenstein represents an interesting example of an
author's mood and talent coinciding with the emotional and
intellectual requirements of large numbers of his contemporaries.

For Samuel Hoffenstein arrived on the scene at a time
when a new kind of American was emerging. Whereas Arthur Guiterman and Oliver Herford smiled at life's foibles
with gentle tolerance, there is in the Hoffenstein verses a
sweet sadness, coupled with a flick of the whip. His work is
uneven—that is, some of his verses are much better than
others—but always in the laughter there is an unmistakable
undercurrent of seriousness, as though he were saying: "I do
not laugh for the fun of it, but because it is necessary if one
is to survive."

And an America already finding the quickening pace of the twentieth century as demanding as it was exciting, agreed with him that the hero does not always triumph; that the ways of man are not always understandable; that the largest questions of life must remain without answers, and that it is therefore more comfortable to gird one's inner sensitivity with the armor of humor.

Samuel Hoffenstein was born in Lithuania, the son of Josiah Mayer and Taube Gita (Kahn) Hoffenstein, who brought him to the United States when he was four. He attended the public schools of Wilkes-Barre, Pennsylvania, and received his higher education at Lafayette College in Easton, Pennsylvania, from which he was graduated in 1911 with a bachelor's degree in philosophy. It is significant that philosophy, the science that investigates the facts and principles of reality and of human nature and conduct, was his major subject, for in all his verse, even the brittlest, there is the feeling of life and man being examined. "Look here," says Hoffenstein in his poems, "I will pinpoint for you how utterly absurd we are, how futile this struggle is," and yet often, the poet that he was overrode this cynicism and conceded the wonders of beauty and love.

For a short time, Hoffenstein was the principal of a Wilkes-Barre public school, but writing appealed to him more than being an educator and, after an apprenticeship as a member of the city staff of the Wilkes-Barre *Times*, he went to New York. He seems to have belonged, by instinct and temperament, to the bustling big city, especially to a growing new giant of a city that was attracting everyone from everywhere, and he wrote with feeling: "I'd rather listen to a flute / In Gotham than a band in Butte."

Hoffenstein brought to the New York of 1912 a wry-mindedness that matched its own, and that of much of the country. At least, the avant-garde of the United States (and perhaps other readers and thinkers) was coming into a new sophistication, was beginning to question many of the adages of *Poor Richard's Almanac,* and the cultural ground of America was ready for a crop of satirical wit. Hoffenstein became a New York *Sun* reporter in that year, a special writer for the same paper in the next year, and its dramatic critic starting with the 1914–15 season. In the articles he wrote under the heading "The Playgoer," he increasingly sensed and satisfied this developing public appetite.

From 1916 to 1927 he was closely affiliated with those areas of New York in which the new cultural moods and movements were being shaped, the "literary set," the newspapers, and the theater. As press agent for the colorful theatrical producer Al Woods, he was, in the words of the editors of *Twentieth Century Authors,* "the creator of various legends about this rough diamond among impresarios." The Hoffenstein thrusts, flare, imagination, cosmopolitanism, and sensitivity to the metropolitan society that was beginning to hustle (even though it may not have been quite sure where it was going) made what he wrote good copy for the daily papers.

The New York Times later commented, "During the middle years of the 1920s, Mr. Hoffenstein was press agent for Mr. Woods and so delightfully witty were his glorifications of his employer's activities that New York drama editors were continually asking for more."

During the latter part of this period, he wrote a column for the New York *Tribune,* a department called "The Dome," and it was through this writing—including a parody of "The Daybook," written by Burton Rascoe, the paper's literary critic, which amused Rascoe—that Hoffenstein was encouraged to produce the book of verse that has become an American literary landmark. For Rascoe found truth and competence in Hoffenstein's commentary on his life and times, and urged him to put together a collection of light verse.

When *Poems in Praise of Practically Nothing* (a title, half casual, half serious, that furnishes a clue to the book's contents) was published in 1928, Burton Rascoe's faith was justified and Hoffenstein's reputation established. Rascoe praised these verses for originality of thought and viewpoint and for their technical perfection; he compared Hoffenstein to the nineteenth-century German poet Heinrich Heine, who also offered in his poems a mastery of rhyme and rhythm, effective use of surprises and contrasts of facetiousness and irony.

The New Yorker magazine described Hoffenstein's style as "the surprise attack, the epigrammatic double-take," and thousands of Americans bought the book eagerly, because they recognized it as a mirror of America 1928.

What kind of an America was it?

Charles A. Lindbergh was still "Lucky Lindy" to the nation because of his trans-Atlantic solo flight the year before. The 18th Amendment was in effect and, offshore, the Coast Guard was busily pursuing rumrunners. A six-room cottage in New England sold for $4,000. President and Mrs. Calvin Collidge went to Andover, Massachusetts, to take part in the sesquicentennial celebration of Phillips Academy; Mr. Coolidge was the first President since George Washington to visit there.

Women's two-piece dresses of wool jersey came with tiered tunics long enough to cover half the skirt. The Bremen flyers, conquerors of the east-west Atlantic air route, were hailed by tremendous crowds in Boston, and the U.S. Marines were fighting rebels in Nicaragua.

And in a New England textile city, 27,000 workers were on strike and 27 mills were idle.

In Chicago, a woman swam in a hotel pool for 50 hours, 10 minutes, 15 and two-fifths seconds, taking only hot chocolate as nourishment, finally breaking the previous endurance record by 17 hours and capturing a $5,000 prize.

Newspaper advertisements noted that a "roomy, five-passenger" Marmon automobile was available for $1,395, and ham was 25 cents a pound.

That was the America of which Hoffenstein sang in a bitter-sweet tone with a light-heavy touch because it too was a paradox: It had promise and poverty; it was exciting and depressing; it was part real and part fairy tale.

Since the nation was obviously on the threshold of a revolutionary era in which its people, once concerned principally with Main Street, were soon enough to find themselves involved with virtually everything everywhere, and on a scale previously unimaginable, how appropriate was Hoffenstein's description of his book: "Songs about life and brighter things yet; a survey of the entire earthly panorama, animal, vegetable and mineral, with appropriate comment by the author of a philosophic, whimsical, humorous or poetic nature—a truly remarkable undertaking!"

There were, then, some almost frantically joyous and breath-taking aspects of American life, but no drowsiness; its daily contrasts did not make for a comfortable time in which to live. Thus, Hoffenstein treated his readers to poetry that shocked, with its juxtaposition of Mobiloils and marigolds, of willow trees and Texaco; it was he who in verse longed for a robin in the grass singing "Socony."

Hoffenstein wrote poems to his own insomnia; he called

himself a "sap" for being a poet, because sensitivity was a burden that gave him neuroses. He mocked mamas who taught their "little lambs" what to do, removed the "hard look" from their eyes, and took them to Ziegfeld to be "glorified," for the beautiful Zeigfeld girl, looked upon as a fabulous creature whose life contained fame, fortune, and excitement, was one of the heroines of the age.

Hoffenstein poked fun at some serious poets, including Vachel Lindsay, with a deftness of imitation and an eye for weaknesses that revealed his own scholarliness. He even mocked the object of his (or of somebody's) love: ". . . your little voice, so soft and kind / Your little soul, your little mind."

He looked at the humpy camel curiously, but noted that it looked back at him just as curiously. Yet underlying this capriciousness was the iron sadness, and he closed the volume by "sheathing the little penny sword," deprecating his own efforts, and concluding, "a . . . lot it matters, either way."

This was the note of the times; he had struck it soundly, and since it was not only the tenor of 1928 but also of the age then unfolding, the so-called Jazz era, an unheard-of thing happened. *Poems in Praise of Practically Nothing* was a "runaway"; 90,000 copies of it were sold in the first six months after publication.

Two years later, Hoffenstein completed *Year In, You're Out*, another collection of verse. Some of its contents had previously been published in such magazines as *Harper's*, *The New Yorker*, *Poetry*, *American Mercury*, and *Vanity Fair*, for he now had a substantial reputation in this field.

This second effort had many brittle bits in it and considerable wisecrackery, and did not receive from the critics praise as unqualified as that given to *Poems in Praise of Practically Nothing*. But it contained a persistent thread of the same feelings, with occasional notes of great poignancy.

Moonlight on the city street, Hoffenstein observed, was like "tired, spent lightning alseep"; he expressed a certain admiration (although offering little hope) for those who try, like little birds, to fly above mountainous walls with "little broken wings of words." He remembered that when he was little, his mother had gone through the kitchen, by the stove in the early morning "heaping warm against the dawn / Little services of love."

Yet, characteristically, he must wield the rapier as well. He noted that trans-Atlantic flights, the weal and woe of his times, had not affected his status in the least respect; he wished he had the indifference of a parrot that does not "care a caw for beast or man."

Although he could not have known it, with these two volumes, two thirds of Hoffenstein's contribution to American light verse had been made. At this time, he changed his way of life abruptly, moving from New York to Los Angeles to write for the motion picture industry. For years, he virtually gave up writing poetry, spending all his time working as a Hollywood scenarist. He remarked laconically, "Poetry doesn't pay off in royalty checks."

Commenting in similar vein on his new profession, he added later, "In the movies, we writers work our brains to the bone and what do we get for it? A lousy fortune." It was this type of remark that led the editors of *Twentieth Century Authors* to observe of Hoffenstein in Hollywood: "His conversation, it is said, is often of sardonic raillery, barbed with the most astonishing word combinations spoken in tones of strained bitterness that makes for him a sort of vocal sanctuary against the world."

His career in Hollywood was marked by association with several outstanding motion pictures. He prepared the screen adaptation of Theodore Dreiser's *An American Tragedy*. He was co-author of the screen plays *Sentimental Journey*, *Cluny Brown*, and *His Butler's Sister*, all appearing in 1946, and of many earlier film scenarios, including the version of *The Phantom of the Opera* in which Nelson Eddy starred in 1943.

All of this time, the small magic of his verse retained its popular appeal. In early 1947, fourteen years after Hoffenstein moved to California, Franklin Pierce Adams (F.P.A.) reviewed an anthology of Hoffenstein poetry for *The New York Times*, and concluded that "a rereading of Hoffenstein is a reminiscent joy and it is a voyage of discovery to a generation unable to read twenty years ago."

Two days before his 57th birthday, in the early morning, Samuel Hoffenstein was stricken with a heart attack in his Los Angeles home. He retained consciousness long enough to phone two physicians; they arrived to find him dead.

His last book of light verse, *Pencil in the Air*, was published three days after his death; one of its reviewers noted that, although Hoffenstein had said that poetry "doesn't pay off," *Poems in Praise of Practically Nothing* had sold nearly 200,000 copies since 1928.

Thus ended the life, but certainly not the impact upon the literature of our times, of the man of whom poet William Rose Benét once said, "At his best, he can be gorgeously biting," yet [he] also was capable of writing tenderly, "The heart's dead are never buried."

> Little by little we subtract
> Faith and Fallacy from Fact,
> The Illusory from the True,
> And starve upon the residue.
> —*Rag-Bag*

DONALD ROBERT PERRY
MARQUIS

[1878–1937]

I<small>T WOULD BE</small> one on me if I should be remembered longest for creating a cockroach character," Don Marquis (pronounced Markwis) remarked ruefully in 1932 after the unsuccessful opening of his religious play, *The Dark Hours*, on which he had labored ten years.

Yet this is precisely what has happened, for Don Marquis, successful newspaper columnist turned author, is linked inextricably and tenderly by thousands of readers to archy, the indomitable cockroach (whose writings were typed without capital letters because he could not reach the shift key on the typewriter) and to mehitabel, archy's hoydenish cat friend.

This irony is a reflection of the life of Don Marquis, humorist, dramatist, and poet, for he brought laughter to many, yet experienced tragedy and disappointment. Even his writing, which seemed to flow effortlessly, was pecked out in one-finger style, and he once told an audience of Yale students that he wrote in "an agony" of effort.

He was born, not only on the day of a total eclipse of the sun, but during the actual eclipse. By coincidence, he was

61

being interviewed in 1925 during another solar eclipse and the interviewer mentioned the "queer sort of impression our total eclipse" was making that day "on the public." Marquis smiled and replied, "Being born during a total eclipse has made me feel that eclipses are nothing much. I mean to say that I consider *my* eclipse the great eclipse and one that gets any attention from me has got to live up to it."

If he meant, facetiously, that it would have to produce another Don Marquis, that approaches the realm of the totally impossible.

Marquis was born in Walnut Bureau County, Illinois, a community that he said "helps the C.B. and Q. Railroad keep two cornfields separated." After graduation from Walnut High School, he attended Knox College in Galesburg, Illinois, for a year, but left school to become foreman of a section gang on the Illinois Central Railroad.

At 18, he began producing poetry for the Walnut *Mail and Express*, and also set type for that newspaper. During the next few years, his jobs included schoolteaching, plucking chickens, selling sewing machines, clerking in a drugstore, cultivating corn, and writing poems in support of William Jennings Bryan, Nebraska lawyer, politician, and orator, and Democratic presidential candidate in 1896.

At about this time, Marquis went to Washington, which proved important to his career. There are two versions as to how this came about. One claims that his Bryan poems were so obnoxious to local Republicans that one of them got him a job in the Census Bureau in Washington. Marquis is quoted as saying (obviously with tongue in cheek, if he did say it) that the job offer was "a plot of Mark Hanna [then an influential Republican party leader] to stifle me politically."

The other version holds that Marquis got the job because

he wrote editorials in support of the local representative to Congress, which may very likely have been the case. However, the important thing was the move itself.

In Washington, he attended art school and worked as a largely unpaid reporter for the Washington *Times*, a task to which he brought, among other qualities, a painful shyness. During this period, he was assigned to interview the author Booth Tarkington. Tarkington was then a young writer whose play *Monsieur Beaucaire*, based on a novel of his own that first appeared serially in *McClure's* magazine, was beginning to attract widespread attention. As Marquis recalled the interview, there was an initial silence, finally broken with the timid question: "Is this your first play, Mr. Tarkington?"

"Yes," replied Tarkington, offering him a cigarette.

After they had smoked one of Tarkington's extra-long cigarettes and the silence was becoming acute, Marquis made another effort: "Do you like the play, Mr. Tarkington?"

"Yes," said Tarkington.

Then followed an even longer and much more painful silence, before Marquis succeeded in asking his final question: "How did you come to write the play, Mr. Tarkington?"

In reply, Tarkington sighed very deeply and shook his head. "I don't know," he said, "I don't—know." Whereupon, with this fund of information, young Mr. Marquis took his departure.

Nevertheless, Marquis decided to become a serious newspaperman; he eventually went to Atlanta, where he worked on the *Journal*, and soon became an editorial writer at a salary of $18 a week. He had always been interested in the stage, but turned down an opportunity to act, at $3 a week less than his newspaper salary, because "I decided to stay where the big money was."

From the Atlanta *Journal*, he went to the editorship of Joel Chandler Harris's *Uncle Remus* magazine, and it was while editing this publication that he met his first wife, Reina Melcher, also a writer, when she came to submit a manuscript to him.

They were married in 1909, moved to New York, and had dreary financial struggles until he began to conduct "The Sun Dial," his column in the New York *Sun*. The publication of his first book, *Danny's Own Story*, in 1912 brought forth reviews that compared Don Marquis to Mark Twain and established him as an American humorist of the first rank.

This book was the first of many best sellers that Marquis produced over the next twenty-four years. But it was in his column, first in the *Sun* and later in the New York *Herald-Tribune*, where it was called "The Lantern," that he began to reach the thousands who chuckled at the witty characters of his creation. In addition to archy and mehitabel, there were such personalities as The Old Soak, a vehicle for Marquis's antipathy toward the 18th Amendment—not because of any personal fondness for alcohol, but because of his deep dislike for the prohibitive principle; Hermione and her little group of Serious Thinkers, who satirized what Marquis saw as the follies of feminine pseudo culture; Captain Peter Fitzurse, the unconquerable raconteur; and Fothergill Finch, master of the beautiful gesture.

Typical of the rapierlike Marquis approach was this reference to Hermione: "She whom Prince Platitude has kissed / You threaten her with night and sorrow? / Slay her by thousands, friend—but list! / More 'little groups' will rise tomorrow."

By 1917, Christopher Morley found Marquis "stout, ruddy

FRANKLIN
PIERCE ADAMS

Wide World Photos

RICHARD ARMOUR

Wide World Photos

MARGARET FISHBACK

Wide World Photos

ARTHUR
GUITERMAN

Underwood & Underwood

OLIVER HERFORD

SAMUEL
HOFFENSTEIN

Los Angeles Times Photo

DON MARQUIS

Wide World Photos

PHYLLIS McGINLEY

Wide World Photos

CHRISTOPHER MORLEY

OGDEN NASH

DOROTHY PARKER

BERT
LESTON TAYLOR

Chicago Tribune Photo

JAMES
WHITCOMB RILEY

and fond of cigars, dark beer and sausages. He looks like a blend of Falstaff and Napoleon III. He begins to stand out as one of the most penetrating satirists and resonant scoffers at folderol that this continent holds. But he is far more than a columnist; he is a poet, a kind of . . . Meredith, with a dash of Eugene Field."

Marquis's imagination set him apart; how many would dare try to make a likable hero of a cockroach? The quality of his workmanship was outstanding. Sometimes he would spend a day or two polishing a line, even though he once remarked wistfully, "Publishing a volume of verse is like dropping a rose leaf into a canyon and waiting to hear the echo."

Yet he persisted. In praise of his work, his friend Morley said, "Don Marquis can turn a rondeau or a triolet as gracefully as a bank clerk can roll Durham cigarettes. His are potent, yeasty verses fashioned from the roaring loom of every day. . . . He sings and celebrates a robust world where men struggle upward from the slime, and discontent leaps from star to star."

Marquis's first play and his greatest stage hit (He wrote it in three days, saying afterward, "I had taken the check in advance; I *had* to write it") was called *The Old Soak*, a tear-stained piece based on characters he had made popular in his column. The leading role was later played by Wallace Beery, in a motion-picture version. The play was sentimental, humorous nonsense; it was also a Broadway hit that, according to *The New York Times*, brought the author $85,000.

By 1925, when Dorothea Lawrance Mann of the Boston *Evening Transcript* interviewed this man of contrast and versatility, his friends included, among many other men of eminence, William Rose Benét, Heywood Broun, Franklin P. Adams, Walter Hampden, and Grantland Rice. She found

that Marquis possessed "something of the leonine quality
. . . He is modeled on a large scale, and makes considerable
effort to keep it from getting larger . . . He has a broad
mouth which can smile, though it does not too often."

With a certain plaintiveness, Marquis said of his size: "I
would like to be skinny. I have always had an idea that my
soul is slender. I can walk through a baker's shop, smell
bread cooking and put on two pounds. I have always wanted
to be tall, slender and handsome, with a blond mustache."

At 47, this man who said that normally he was serious, but
had surrendered to the thesis that America expects fat men to
be funny and amiable, was writing an average of a thousand
words a day, three hundred thousand a year. Over the three
previous years, he had written one million words, equal to
ten full-length novels of average size. In that time he had also
written three plays. Of all this, he said simply: "I work like a
son of a gun."

The broad range of Marquis's poetry was extraordinary.
On one day he could write in his column: "Hell is full of
fiddlers. / Dogs are full of fleas. / And I'm as full of notions
/ As the grippe is full of sneeze. / Here's a column of them /
You can read them if you please. / Maybe some are caviar /
Maybe some are cheese."

And on another day he could ponder: "Is life itself not
wonder-worth that we must cry for miracles? Is it not
strange enough we breathe . . . ?"

He could have archy say candidly, "i never think at all
when i write. / nobody can do two things at the / same time
/ and do them well."

And in virtually the next breath, Marquis's lines to a lost
love cry out poignantly, "Only the dust is here, thy dust /
But when chill May uncloses / Her petals and is June, I feel

/ A heartbeat shake the roses."

Of his writing experience, he recalled that he sold the first short story he ever wrote. "I wrote it on Monday, sent it off on Tuesday, and a week later, got a check for $50 for it," he said. Then he added: "It was two years before I sold another. It was discouraging. The thought can't help occurring that the first one must have been accident." Somewhat similarly, his first play was accepted before he wrote it, and was overwhelmingly successful; the others were failures.

Reviewing the first dozen years of his writing career in New York (he had had twelve books published during this period), Marquis concluded, "There isn't much to me except my books. If there is anything that is interesting to the American public, it is what I have written. I have never been anywhere, never done anything. I've been chained to a desk. Might just as well have been in the hardware business so far as any romance or excitement, or anything of that sort is concerned."

But his followers thought much more of him, and of his abilities. They were moved by the sad beauty of his seriousness; delighted by the mirth of his burlesque and titillated by his gift for preposterous association, such as: "Henry married, Hoke Smith in the Senate, Euripedes dead . . . how Time flies!"

Benjamin De Casseres, newspaper columnist and poet, accepting the constant conflict of tears and laughter within Marquis, called him "Shelley trying to lasso the Golden Calf; a born poet and bitter satirist." Sir Hugh Walpole, English novelist, found his humor "utterly and unmistakably American."

Marquis neither felt nor found any incongruity in the fact that his drama of Holy Week, *The Dark Hours*, on which he worked a decade during the last years of his professional productivity, inevitably had to stand in the minds of many as written by the author of *The Old Soak* and the creator of archy, the unconquerable cockroach. Unquestionably, this was because, dissimilar as the vehicles and their characters were, he felt that the vein of truth was in all of them. Of their differences, however, he remarked, "I have come to the conclusion that I will not try to do anything for the stage that hasn't got a little beauty in it. Newspaper work is a meal ticket, but anything outside of that should be serious stuff with beauty in it."

Of *The Dark Hours*, he said, during the period in which he was working on it, "I have tried merely to give the orthodox religious version of what happened that night, to present it as an acting play, to eliminate everything that did not tend toward this idea, and to take no sides in the matter whatever. It was an amazing night, that night before the Crucifixion; things happened every few minutes."

Dorothea Mann, who had had an opportunity to read some of the script before its unsuccessful presentation to the public, praised its "austere beauty" and wrote that she was "inclined to think this is the greatest triumph of his career." Several writers since have suggested that the play's failure many have been due to many circumstances unrelated to its quality.

Marquis's first wife died in 1923, and in 1926 he married Marjorie Vonnegut, a former Theater Guild actress. At about this time, he ceased writing a newspaper column; in 1923, the New York *Tribune* hired him for $20,000 a year, a large salary then, but Marquis, who said writing a column was "like digging a grave" for himself every day, chose not to continue with the newspaper after its merger with the

Herald in 1924.

Devoting himself to other writing, he produced, in addition to magazine contributions, 11 volumes of prose and poetry between 1927 and 1935, among them *Love Sonnets of a Cave Man, When the Turtles Sing,* and *archy and mehitabel.* During the latter part of this period, however, the burdens of life, including poor health, began to weigh heavily upon him.

In 1929, he suffered a slight heart attack; in 1932, a brain hemorrhage left him totally blind for a time, and in 1936 he was stricken by the major cerebral hemorrhage that left him a helpless invalid, unable to speak to the many friends who flocked to visit him.

In November, 1930, Lee Shippey wrote in the Los Angeles *Times:* "Marquis has known all the trials which embitter some men, bereavement, dangerous illness, haunting fear for the health of his little daughter [Barbara] and financial worry. But through all of them, geniality or a kind of sublime faith, has made him lovable and humorous, and so he has come through to success and the affection of all literary America."

The "success and affection of all literary America" of which Mr. Shippey wrote were proved demonstrably. In 1923, Don Marquis was honored by election to the National Institute of Arts and Letters. And in 1936, after his paralytic stroke, four of his friends wrote, under his name, a story, "Tablecloth," which they sold to the *Saturday Evening Post* and later to Paramount for production as a motion picture. The four ghost writers were Patterson NcNutt, Gene Fowler, Grover Jones, and Nunnally Johnson. The checks went to Don Marquis.

But a year later, permanently bedridden and unable to

write, Don Marquis, once so full of vigor, was described by *Newsweek* magazine as a "penniless and hopeless cripple." So died an American humorist whose writings have been compared to those of Ambrose Bierce and Stephen Crane. Hilaire Belloc said: (concerning Marquis's piece about the parrot in the Mermaid Tavern), "It is a permanent addition to the furniture of the mind."

The man of whom it was written, "He never was known to do a mean thing or to speak ill of anyone" was dead; yet, as he had predicted, the indomitable cockroach and the hoydenish cat went on and on, and still do. Seventeen years after Don Marquis died, the editors of *Twentieth Century Authors* noted: " 'Archy and Mehitabel,' a short jazz opera by George Kleinsinger, based on Marquis's sketches, was produced in New York, and later recorded, with considerable success."

> dance mehitabel dance
> caper and shake a leg
> what little blood is left
> will fizz like wine in a keg.
> —*the song of mehitabel*

PHYLLIS MCGINLEY

[1905–   ]

PHYLLIS MC GINLEY, in private life Mrs. Charles L. Hayden, once offered a typically forthright evaluation of her substantial contribution to American letters:

"I know every technical trick, but I don't quite reach the plateau of the great poets—Eliot, Auden, Yeats—poets whose genius is so great I could weep over them.

"I have one facet of genius, and only one. I have an infinite capacity for taking pains. My passion is for lucidity, and I don't mean simple-mindedness. If people can't understand it, why write it? Swift [Jonathan Swift, English satirist] read his stuff to the stable boys.

"I do think I have been a useful person. At a time when poetry has become the property of the universities and not the common people, I have a vast number of people who have become my readers. I have kept the door open and perhaps led them into greater poetry."

The "vast number" of readers is measurable; in approximately ten years, *The Love Letters of Phyllis McGinley* sold 80,000 copies, and in less than four years, *Times Three*, an anthology of her poetry, sold 60,000 in the hard cover edition alone. Undoubtedly, her readership numbers more women than men, for in her poetry she extols her role in the home, as wife and mother, and thus do many of her followers identify with the McGinley temporary frustrations and permanent joys.

The phrase "permanent joys" is not to suggest that Miss McGinley is "too light-hearted, too adjusted" to be taken seriously, as a reviewer once concluded, for her approach to life is a reasonable balance of sugar and salt. She could write, "Praise youth for toppling the idols, breaking leases," and in another vein remark: "For the young, if they're kept out of sight, I've a great deal of forbearance."

Further, Phyllis McGinley's stature as a poet of merit and meaning is well established. W. H. Auden, the eminent American poet, has commented: "There is a certain way of writing, which one calls light, but underneath, it can carry a great depth of emotion. Where do you place a work like Pope's *Rape of the Lock?* You could equally call it light verse or marvelous poetry. . . .

"What, in fact, distinguishes Miss McGinley's poems from those of most light-verse poets is that no man could have written them; in contrast, the feminine imagination accepts facts, and is coolly realistic."

In describing her theory of "keeping the door open" to poetry, Phyllis McGinley has also said that one of her aims has been to "narrow the gulf between light and serious verse." She must have felt a sense of achievement in this direction when she was awarded the Pulitzer Prize for poetry in 1961; it was the first time that a writer of light verse had been thus honored. The award was given for *Times Three,* selected verse from three decades, and included poems written through the 1930s, 1940s, and 1950s.

The contents of the prize volume range from a malediction

on the people who built a house across the street, obscuring her favorite view ("Down went the lilies' yellow glory / and up their sordid second story") to the rigors of swimming in Maine's chill waters; from an observation that the so-called independent may have no opinion at all, to a defense of marriage as opposed to a nine-to-five job "in some tall town," in which she concluded, as a housewife and mother, "It's very clear I might have done much worse."

It would be a great mistake to label Phyllis McGinley, who is a member of the National Institute of Arts and Letters and recipient of the Edna St. Vincent Millay Memorial Award of the Poetry Society of America, as simply a somewhat lonely champion of hearth, home, and housewifery. (Sales of her books would suggest that she is not even lonely.)

Certainly, for thirty years or so she has written with obvious pleasure of motherhood and domesticity, yet she is no more an ordinary wife and mother than she is an ordinary poet, and her message is not "marriage versus career," but, more broadly, the proposition that today's educated woman can fit happily into the framework of the home.

Miss McGinley told *Time* magazine in 1965, "Of course, women have a right to work if they can do so without stinting the family.

"I have nothing at all against housewives who use their education and their brains outside the home. I have, from time to time, used mine. By and large though, the world runs better when men and women keep to their own spheres.

"But more important, we who belong to the profession of housewife hold the fate of the world in our hands. It is our influence which will determine the culture of the coming generations. We are the people who chiefly listen to the music, buy the books, attend the theater, prowl the art galleries, collect for the charities, brood over the schools, converse with the children. Our minds need to be rich and flexible for these duties."

The product of German and Irish stock, Phyllis McGinley was born in Ontario, Oregon, the daughter of Daniel and Julia (Kiesel) McGinley, and her early experiences contain adequate clues as to how and why she became a poet known for her praise of the home.

Because her father dealt in land, requiring frequent moves, there was an inevitable rootlessness during her childhood years. At one point, the McGinleys lived on a ranch in Colorado, and because of its remoteness (even the country school had only two or three pupils, and sometimes her mother was the teacher), Phyllis turned to books for companionship. The scope and depth of her reading, even as early as the age of ten, were extraordinary; fortunately, although the family was not wealthy, good books were available to her and the imprint of this scholarship is everywhere present in her verse.

Although the verse she composed when six years old may not be outstanding compared to what she was able to create later, it offers a revealing portrait of a child who was sensitive and thoughtful and, happily for American letters, forced by lack of playmates and extracurricular activities to develop her inner resources. She wrote then: "Sometimes in the evening / When the sky is blue and pink / I love to lie in the hammock / And think and think and think."

Not yet in her teens when her father died, Phyllis next lived in Ogden, Utah, in a home shared by her mother and aunt. Ogden had been the residence of her mother's family when they came to this country from Germany, and here

Phyllis attended Ogden High School and the Sacred Heart Academy; later, she went to the University of Utah in Salt Lake City.

After graduation from college, she taught one year in Ogden, then came east to teach high-school English in New Rochelle, New York, where she remained four and a half years, writing poetry in her spare time.

Although her poetry attracted favorable editorial attention, its "sad, Swinburne-ish" touch (her own description) in no way set her apart from other women poets in America, whose rhymed messages were in the same mood. At the suggestion of a magazine editor, Phyllis McGinley lightened her song, and its brighter approach quickly brought her success.

Professional acceptance of her verse by leading magazines and newspapers brought an immediate result: At the end of the class year, she resigned from her teaching position, and turned to free-lance writing. Moving to New York, she first worked as a copy writer for an advertising agency, and later became poetry editor of *Town and Country* magazine. Meanwhile, she was producing an increasing amount of the light and warm rhymings on life that have become the McGinley trademark.

Marriage in 1936 to Charles Hayden produced a home in suburbia (eventually in Weston, Conn.) for the woman who, since childhood, had wanted the sense of belonging that a home and family can provide. She responded to her new life, including the birth of two daughters, Julie and Patsy, with delight and enthusiasm, and shed no tears for the years when she had dwelt "unfettered in my single flat / My life my own."

Hers now was a world of "leeward-leaning birches," Victorian architecture, and domesticity, but, more than this, there was also the whole richness and sharing of daily experiences in and for the household. It is her zest in expressing this aspect of her life, her buoyant philosophical attitude toward its responsibilities and bounties, her conviction that books and brownies, sonnets and stews are compatible, that has endeared her to so many. Always, her family has come first, but because she has what one critic described as "a high level of competence, an outstanding capacity for self-expression and iron-willed discipline," she has been able to write her poetry in the bits and pieces of time that remain her own. ·

Nor is it fair to suggest that her poems are simply about suburban life and family activities, that there is no more to them than delight and an unusual sense of intimate communication between author and reader. Many of her verses are concerned with social criticism, and the following, entitled "Hostess," is an excellent example of Phyllis McGinley's deadly aim:

"Games, shower of words to break up tête-á-tête / Desperately bent on stirring up a scheduled merriment / No calm must fall, however brief and narrow / Lest, to her dread / From some small knothole of silence, some hidden burrow / The scotched snake, Thought, should rear its venomed head."

Disciplined efficiency, whether in the preparation of dinner for family or guests or in the punctual meeting of a publisher's deadline (for which she has an excellent reputation), underlies the success of her "double life"; if there are those who subscribe to the thesis that good poets have to be eccentric, Phyllis McGinley is not one of them. Because she labors painstakingly over her writing, she has tended not to think of herself as prolific; yet from 1934 to 1954 she produced fifteen volumes of verse. In addition, she has written several children's books and a collection of essays, entitled *Province of the Heart*, of which *The New York Times Book Review* said in 1959, "It talks back to those who have patronized, satirized, psychoanalyzed or social science-ized surburban life."

Miss McGinley, who once observed that "gluttony is the last lovely sin left for the middle-aged" is obviously appreciative of good food insofar as it relates to the good life, but her message is far broader and deeper. In an interview with Vivian Brown of the Associated Press, at the McGinley home in Connecticut, the author made these remarks:

"Are we going back to the medieval thesis that education unfits a woman to change diapers or make lemon meringue pie? Does appreciation of good poetry or language cripple a girl's talent for making chocolate cake?

"Often, because the seeds of discontent have been planted, a wife will feel she is doomed to drudgery if she isn't out in the working world with her husband. What she doesn't realize is that she will probably be just another working woman anyway, whereas in the home, she can win rewards out of all proportion to her husband, who never can approach such triumphs.

"I regret that many girls of this generation can't run up a hem or cook a meal, although they have been taught to ski, typewrite, sail a boat and define Einstein."

Some of Phyllis McGinley's most sensitive and successful verse, clearly inspired by her own family, has concerned the painful and pleasurable age of adolescence. For example, few are likely to surpass in poignant truth her observations that thirteen "is the one age that defeats the metaphor," because it is neither town nor city, has neither wit nor power, has secrets even from itself, and "admits none to the terrors that it feels."

Miss McGinley shuns the limelight and likes to live "quietly and peacefully," but fame often brings demands with it. In 1965, she was one of two poets (the other was Mark Van Doren) invited to the White House and asked to recite one of her poems as part of the Festival of the Arts.

She read one originally written for a Columbia University commencement, adding six lines to fit the White House occasion. In it she said, "Let us, for once, praise presidents / Providing dream its festival hour / And while the pot of culture's bubblesome / Praise poets, even when they're troublesome."

In recent years, she has written more prose than poetry, principally for national magazines, and generally on domestic subjects. She also wrote the lyrics for a musical revue, *Small Wonder* (1948), and the narration for the film *The Emperor's Nightingale* (1951).

> Nurses can cure you, nurses restore you
> But nurses are bound that they'll do things for you
> They run with eggnogs from hither and thither
> They fling out your flowers before they wither
> They fetch your breakfast at dawn's first crack
> They keep on pleading to rub your back
> With eau de cologne they delight to slosh you
> And over and over, they want to wash you.
> *—In a Hospital: Message found in a bottle*
> *thrown from a window at Harkness Pavilion*

CHRISTOPHER DARLINGTON
MORLEY

[1890–1957]

How DID my baby fingers first close upon the pen?" mused Christopher Morley in 1925. "At the age of seven, my family was traveling in Germany and I wrote at great length 'The Traveling Morleys,' which my mother still cherishes, along with an impressive serial entitled 'The Adventures of a Woodcutter,' which I used to relate to the other children at school.

"At Haverford [Haverford College, Pennsylvania], I wrote my first poem that was printed. It was called 'To a Skull' and ended, 'One thing at least is sure, and that is death.' "

Christopher Morley was born at Haverford, the son of Dr. Frank Morley, an English Quaker and professor of mathematics, and Lilian Janet (Bird) Morley, also English by birth, a gifted musician and poet. During Christopher Morley's childhood and youth, his father taught both at Haverford and at Johns Hopkins University in Baltimore; young Morley was eventually graduated from Haverford in 1910, a member of Phi Beta Kappa, with a baccalaureate thesis on

Robert Louis Stevenson and the award of the Maryland Rhodes Scholarship to Oxford University, England.

The three years at Oxford's New College were very important in shaping what Morley (who once described his early life as "an Anglo-American capsule") was to become. First, a British magazine bought a poem of his, entitled "A Yellow Rose," paying him a shilling for it. There also appeared a slender volume of verse, *The Eighth Sin*, by Morley, concerning which his New College tutor, Herbert Fisher, remarked, "The chief advantage of writing poetry in youth is that it improves one's prose style in old age."

Many years later, Morley recalled: "Oxford was still Arcadia (that is, a place of simple, quiet pleasures) before the First World War. . . . Now my young brothers are immersed in current problems. Women? Oh, yes, I remember some. They used to sit modestly in the corners, away from the fire. Those big halls were cold."

Of his senior year in the winter of 1912–13, he had a story to tell: "I was taking a course in constitutional law given by that grand man Grant Robertson. I was a little late at the first lecture and it was just by chance I saw a vacant seat down front and slid into it. I soon discovered that I was next the Prince of Wales.

"He was a delightful, appealing, attractive and charming youth, but after eighteen years of private tutors, he was hopelessly lost trying to follow Robertson, who was a rapid lecturer. Toward the end of the lecture, he began to look wistfully at my notes, so I let him take them. He kept taking them, all through the course, although he began to learn the note business before he got through with it."

In 1936, after Prince Edward had ascended to the throne of England, Christopher Morley commented, "I dare say the king knows more about constitutional law now than I ever did."

After Oxford, he came home steerage on the *Mauretania*. In England, he had met Helen Booth Fairchild (who was to become his wife the next year, 1914), and he described himself as being "filled with a high moral and literary sense of romance."

F. N. Doubleday, head of the New York publishing firm, Doubleday, Paige, whom Morley referred to as "Effendi" (a Turkish title of respect, meaning Chief, Sir, or Master), took pleasure in relating how Morley got his first job. Said Frank Doubleday, "The first time I ever saw Christopher Morley, he was delightfully young, with an enthusiasm which was very appealing. He thought, as others have, that the most delightful way to earn his living would be to become part of a publishing house.

"He said, 'I want a job and I want it here, and I hope right now,' not with the air of a life insurance agent, but with the eagerness of a thirsty soul with refreshment in sight.

"Finally, I said to him, 'If you had your choice of any job in the place, which one would you choose?'

"Without a second's hesitation, he answered, 'Yours.'

"I felt that any youngster who was so eager to assume the burden of a somewhat complicated life might be encouraged. So I told him to hang up his coat and hat, put him at a desk, and told him to go to work."

Morley performed many functions in the publishing business; one of them was helping during the Christmas rush at the Old Corner Bookstore in Boston. In a newspaper column, he wrote: "For four years, we served as an extra hand at the Old Corner. One of our greatest treasures is an unsolicited testimonial from old Dick Fuller, the head of the store, saying, 'You certainly are a born salesman,' which he gave to us because, he said, it would be useful to us in hunting another job.

"We recall, for instance, how we ventured to recommend some work on philosophy to a charmingly esoteric-looking customer and found him to be Josiah Royce [the American philosopher]. Or how we tried to sell something to Miss Amy Lowell [the eminent American poet and literary critic] and she swept implacably onward to her favorite salesman. If you have never seen high-spirited Bostonians buying books just before Christmas, little you know to what fire and frenzy the literate passion can rise.

"It was standing over a radiator at the front of the store (before open for business) that we first read Vachel Lindsay's 'General Booth,' which (in Sir Philip Sidney's grand phrase) stirred us more than a trumpet."

When this column of Morley's was published in a Boston newspaper, "old Dick Fuller" commented, "Yes, we have happy memories of Morley's sojourn here, but it is not a matter of record or tradition that he was ever on hand before the hour of opening the store for business."

In 1915, Mr. and Mrs. Morley went to spend a fortnight's vacation at an old farmhouse in Pike County, Pennsylvania. It rained all the time they were there. After reading all the books, together and separately, and writing sermons to each other to while away the time, as did the Pilgrims en route to America ("Oh, yes," said Morley, "they crossed the ocean in a hum of sermonizing"), he started *Parnassus on Wheels*, reading the chapters to Mrs. Morley to amuse her.

What its principal character, Roger, has to say, reveals much of Christopher Morley himself: "When you sell a man a book, you sell him a whole new life; a good book, like Eve, ought to come from somewhere near the third rib; there ought to be a heart vibrating in it." *Parnassus* was published in 1917 and remains one of the best known of Morley's many works.

With their children, one son and three daughters, Mr. and Mrs. Morley lived on Long Island in a "little house" in what he called a "green escape." His *Songs for a Little House* is a splendid sharing of this life; it and many other of his writings reveal the joy he derived from home and family. He wrote with the insight born of love of the "sloomy and impassive faces" of tadpoles swimming in a milk bottle (observed for a week only, and released); of the dog Gissing (named for George Robert Gissing, English novelist), who tried to poke his nose under water and bark at the same time, "with much coughing and smother."

Christopher Morley knew well and understood the child's need to carry a horse chestnut, a picture of a mouse, and a handkerchief embroidered with a teddy bear when going on a journey, even though none was looked at. Of his house, which he praised for being small, he said, "I'm glad the hovering butterflies feel free to come inside," and he thought it would be dreary to live in a home where faucets do not drip, there is no weather stripping, and neither mice nor children raid the pantry.

His home was a sanctuary; in one of his poems, he wrote, "When I elope with an autumn day and make my green escape. . . ." He noted: "I have to fit my movements into the intervals of the Long Island Railroad. As a result, I never go to town except for the meetings of the Book-of-the-Month Club committee, and to visit the delightful little Italian barber on 46th Street who trims my beard."

"In 1917, Karl Harriman asked me one day if I knew an

ambitious young man to brighten up a magazine," Morley said to an interviewer eight years later. "I said I knew one personally, so off I went to join the *Ladies' Home Journal*, where I stayed a year."

During that period, he went to work on the Philadelphia *Evening Ledger*, where he wrote editorials and a column called "Whim Whams." This was followed by his affiliation with the New York *Evening Post*, for which he began his column "The Bowling Green," a feature that he later carried over to the *Saturday Review of Literature*. He was a pioneer member of the staff of the latter publication, and remained one of its contributing editors until 1941.

In the early twenties, one of his books was titled *Inward Ho*, and some have suggested that this may be the phrase that best describes the man; for as Morley himself said, "I am not the 'Man with the Hoe,' but the man with the inward ho!"

"I have a tenderness for life," he said, "and a loving kindness for truth, yet the only thing I fear is to die barren, to pass out before bearing my truth and beauty, in honor of this life so splendid. For there is not a day and hour when I do not see more beauty than I can comprehend."

His literary output and his professional energies in general were exceptional. Relatively early in life, Morley established his reputation as editor, critic, and a writer of novels, lyrics, and short stories. He did much, especially through his columns (a typical one was described as "an adventure among books"), to give wider audience to such writers as Joseph Conrad, Logan Pearsall Smith, Hilaire Belloc, Walt Whitman, and Don Marquis.

In 1949, he commented: "It has been my custom for more than thirty years to amuse myself by getting out at least one book a year. This was not done intentionally to annoy anyone. The publishers have made a profit on most of them and 'the trade' was more than kind."

Referring to *Parnassus on Wheels* (1917) and *The Haunted Bookshop* (1919) in the 1950s, Morley noted that they were written "more than thirty years ago and have been continuously in print and sale ever since. That is unusual. As far as the book trade is concerned, they are my memorial."

His best-known novels are *Where the Blue Begins* (1922), *Thunder on the Left* (1925), and *Kitty Foyle* (1939). *Thunder on the Left* concerns some children who spied on grown-up life to see whether it was enjoyable. Morley said the book caused him considerable annoyance—many readers wrote to ask what parts of it meant. "As if that were part of an author's job," he exclaimed. "An imaginative author's job is to give the reader an opportunity to collaborate."

Bookish and sentimental, with great popular appeal from his first volume onward, Christopher Morley was best known as novelist, essayist, and lecturer (he found lecturing "exhausting, exciting, and an immortal experience"), but he preferred to regard himself as a poet. He once said, "I have the horridest feeling that after it is too late for me, someone will really say, 'he wrote poetry.'"

He really did, in keys and colors ranging from the clever lines, "And watch young lovers, breathing hard, / Put heaven on a postal card" to the gentle poem, "No bird has built an April nest / More instinctive than my rhyme, / A hidden coil where thought can rest / In lonely or in stormy time."

Moreover, his outlook was both rural and urban. Of Chicago he wrote, "How do I hold you, city, in the mind . . . / An ocean without salt, a gale roaring / A cruel blackness with a glittering rind." Yet of a country snake he was able to write with equal effectiveness, "In my woodlot, one warm afternoon, / Was a long downward streak, so arrowy and sinuous / It looked continuous . . . / Clean as a flume it sped . . . / And hid unsociable in the honeysuckle brake. . . ."

Throughout, his scholarship rang like a clear bell. Of Alexander Pope (1688–1744), he wrote: "Pope, who loved his rhymes in duplicates / Chose couplets also for his mortal dates: Born '88, precisian to the core / Died, of exactitude, in '44."

As early as 1921, in the fledgling days of radio, Morley was an occasional broadcaster on Station WEAF in New York. But he said, "As soon as I discovered it was going to be profitable, arduous, and involve late-of-nite railroad commuting, I fled. I have always fled from everything that involved steady and rich emoluments.

"I love the early taste of any fine elixir, but as soon as the hoplites come cranking in, I am off with the wind in the willows. I have mapped out the lines of several fortunes for other people, but it would have bored me horribly to consummate them." He once remarked of his verse that "no one can ever say this is a commercial yen," for virtually everything else that he wrote was more lucrative.

In 1928, the New York *Herald-Tribune*'s David Karsner found this man, who was to write approximately fifty books and hundreds of thousands of readable, thoughtful words in other forms, to be " . . . an utterly unselfish person, who affects no poses, wears his clothes loosely . . . whose clear blue eyes flash wisdom and sympathy, whose voice is clear and earnest, whose spirit is not likely to grow old. . . .

"Here is a man who often sits alone far into the night wondering what his dog is dreaming about and who is frequently up before the household is astir, sitting in his room writing, a cup of coffee at his elbow, his pipe lighted. . . . One is impressed instantly with his deep sympathy for all human striving . . . he conceives it to be his business to broadcast ideas and good thinking, with the view of contributing his share to human happiness and enlightenment. I count him one of the most civilized and sensitive men I ever have met. . . ."

The range of his reflection was limitless and exciting. "Many of the mysterious, impalpable things he wants to know," wrote H. F. Manchester, "belong to a realm of thought as yet unequipped with the proper retinue of terminology. He wants to know why a poet writes a poem, what first microscopic germ plasm of unconceived beauty ripens into a sonnet which men repeat with joy in their hearts."

In later years, Morley concluded that "we can't plan life too much. Still, I insist that despite its cruelties, tragedies and futilities, it is beautiful, wonderful and miraculous." Asked to comment on the greatest pleasure he had derived from a lifetime of writing, he said it had come from the friends he had made through writing. This view was reaffirmed posthumously, in an unusual manner.

Four days after his death, a black-bordered advertisement appeared in *The New York Times* and the *Herald-Tribune*. It read: "To whom it may concern, Christopher Morley, who died March 28, 1957, asked his executors to use this space to send my unchanged love to many kind and forbearing friends. Our good adventures and absurdities were not forgotten, nor occasions of beauty and moments of disgust. Especially, I wanted to apologize for so many unanswered letters through so many years. Their messages, of whatever sort, were often in my mind. I had many reasons for gratitude, and I was grateful."

> The man I give toast to
> And praise in this sonnet
> Has never played host to
> A bee in his bonnet.
> Remarkably moderate,
> Thoroughly sane,
> Indeed odd and odder it
> Seems to my brain
> So few are inclined to
> Give heed to his tone
> But still have a mind to
> Fool views of their own.
> The wisdom of Sinai is his by the shelf . . .
> Of course you divine I—allude to Myself.
>   —*The Superman*

OGDEN NASH

[1902–   ]

ONLY Ogden Nash would write verse about a motorist who saw a beautiful girl pedestrian and pursued her for eight blocks before he succeeded in running over her "gently," so that he could obtain her name and address in the newspaper account of the accident.

And only Nash then would write that the girl spurned the motorist, who joined the Foreign Legion, which expelled him because he admitted he liked it.

For the trademarks of Ogden Nash are exaggeration, surprise, absurdity, and what one critic called "all the best and worst rhymes," phrased in fantastically irregular line lengths and skillfully wrapped about a message with which the average reader identifies immediately.

Sometimes Nash's lines contain only a half-dozen words. Sometimes they will gallop on for more than a breathful, and with such end rhymes as cloisters and oysters, Venice and tennis, Gertrude Lawrence and abhorrence, madrigals and amateur theadrigals.

But it is his ideas, of course, concerning as they do the stuff of truth (Nash refers to all his verse as "stuff") that endear him to so many, because through his hundreds of

89

verses, he reveals himself as the symbol of fallible, likeable Everyman. He knows, for example, that the average man would not get far as a Bengal lancer because he is not even heroic enough to cross the street against a red light.

Ogden Nash doesn't think that being a child is much of a pastime because he would hate to be held together with safety pins instead of buttons, suspenders, and belts. He wonders when a violin is a fiddle; and why, when he is about to see something interesting out a train window, a hundred-car freight cuts off his view.

Yet his writing is not limited to froth and whimsy. A reviewer, commenting on one of the seventeen volumes of verse Nash produced between 1931 and 1964, wrote, "He fights for every man the fight which every man is afraid to fight for himself. He comes right out against parsley, little boys, banquets, women's hats, salads and the recent frightening epidemic of girl babies."

Ogden Nash, who says of himself, "I have no private life and no personality," was born in Rye, New York, of Southern parentage. The brother of his great-great-grandfather was General Francis Nash, for whom Nashville, Tennessee, was named. Of North Carolina, Nash says, "I have ten thousand cousins in the state."

He attended Harvard for one year ("where I got just enough of a classical education to interfere with my English"), during 1920–21, and left of his own free will ("I've got the papers to prove it"). Actually, the family fortunes took a turn for the worse and Ogden had to leave school and as he says, "scratch on my own." He first took a teaching job at St. George's School in Newport, Rhode Island, which he had attended. Of this experience, he remarked later, "I lost my entire nervous system carving lamb for a table of 14-year-olds."

His next venture was in New York, as a bond salesman. He sold one bond in two years—"to my godmother." Then he tried composing street-car advertisements at $100 a month for a firm that had previously employed novelist F. Scott Fitzgerald for this task. Said Nash, "I never wrote a car card that appeared in New York City . . . just places like Chillicothe, Ohio."

Finally, he transferred to the advertising department of a New York publishing house, an occupation that lasted only six years, but which inadvertently launched him into the field of rambling verse.

Although as a young man he had failed to sell serious verse, his interest in poetry writing had begun early and remained constant. When he was ten and his older sister was about to be married, he wrote: "The beautiful spring at last is here / And has taken my sister, I sadly fear."

In retrospect, Nash said, "I think in terms of rhyme and have since I was six." He almost fell in love with a lady named Mrs. Blorange. She fascinated him because of the similarity of her name to orange, which, like the words "silver" and "pilgrim," have no dictionary rhymes. Also, he favors poetry to prose because "you can say things which, if said in prose, would result in tar and feathers."

Even so, he considers himself a poet by accident, one who started scribbling verse one afternoon when he felt foolish. He wrote something called "Spring Comes to Murray Hill," which related: "I sit in an office at 244 Madison Avenue / And say to himself, you have a responsible job, havenue?" He threw it in the waste basket, retrieved it, sent it to *The*

New Yorker magazine, and it was published. Twenty-eight years later, Nash estimated that he had written 50,000 published lines of verse.

In 1931, after publication of his first book, *Hard Lines* (in which he pointed out that "like an art lover looking at the / Mona Lisa in the Louvre is the New York *Herald-Tribune* / Looking at Mr. Herbert Houvre"), Nash still insisted that the "whole thing is an accident" and disclaimed any originality of thought at all. But the public, which became acquainted with him through *The New Yorker* and the radio quiz show "Information Please," thought otherwise and insisted on adoring him.

At one point, Nash said, "I often wonder whether I'll get tired of writing them [his verses] before the public gets tired of reading them, or whether it will happen the other way. They are just thoughts that must occur to many thousands of men like me who are annoyed by affectation, chauvinism, and intolerance and still are too lazy to do anything about it. Really, they're very platitudinous. You know, you can make almost any platitude sound humorous in verse."

On June 7, 1931, the Associated Press filed the following report from Baltimore: "Wrote Ogden Nash in the introductory couplet of his latest book, 'What shall I do with so and so / She won't say yes and she won't say no.' So and so, otherwise Miss Frances Leonard, said yes today without qualification and became the bride of Nash. . . .

"Nash declined to admit that Miss Leonard was the inspiration of the book (their engagement was announced not long after it was published), but his friends said there was no doubt of it. She is the granddaughter of the late Governor and Mrs. E. E. Jackson of Maryland."

Once described as a "soft-voiced, hazel-eyed six-footer

with a habitual expression of absent-minded inquiry," Ogden Nash is a painstaking craftsman who has done much of his writing in pencil on sheets of yellow paper. For years, he has written at home, because "there are so many interruptions there. I like interruptions. Neither the ideas nor the rhymes come easily. Writing is hard work. The Lord doesn't usually deliver everything to you in one package, as a rule."

Poetry remained his pride and joy ("and my bread and butter," he recalled), but after he became established as a writer of light verse, Hollywood beckoned, and he went west.

"When I first went there," he said, "they locked me up with another chap for six weeks. The project was to convert a book into a movie, but pretty soon the producer went off to New York and forgot all about it. So for two years, they took up my option every time it fell due and gave me a raise and I did nothing whatever." The proceeds enabled Mr. and Mrs. Nash to take a trip to Europe, but eventually, he returned to the East Coast and continued his verse-writing.

In 1943, he wrote the lyrics for Kurt Weill's major Broadway triumph, *One Touch of Venus*. The Weill-Nash comments on this successful partnership are interesting. Nash said: "I approached song writing with the feeling that the impact of the composition has to be instantaneous and direct, and recognition has to be immediate. The listener has to be impressed almost immediately or else he tosses it off. If the same verse were to appear in a book or a magazine, he would have time to digest it more slowly or reread it until he got the message."

Kurt Weill said: "He's a guy who has to feel a pencil squirming in his fingers. Every word counts."

Although Nash produces painstakingly, he is not incapable

of spur-of-the-moment rhymes. Speaking in Worcester, Massachusetts, at a formal affair, he forgot his evening shoes and borrowed those of his host, Dr. Loring Holmes Dodd. When Nash rose to speak, he remarked, "If Professor Dodd were to be struck down by lightning tonight, which God forbid, I want you to understand that his shoes can be filled. I have them on." As he sat down at the table, Nash passed Dodd a slip of yellow paper on which was written: "I raise my glass to Dr. Dodd / By whom many are called, but few are shod."

On lecture tours, he developed a keen respect for his fellow man which undoubtedly was reflected in the wealth of insight to be found in his poems. Nash remarked of his experiences on the lecture circuit, "I found none of this yokelism you sometimes hear complaints about. They're very sincere." His television appearances in the fifties (on "Masquerade Party," for example) also increased his following. Of TV, Nash commented, "I am now recognized by my candy store man when I go to buy a newspaper. Of course, it's not all smooth sailing.

"For one thing, it costs me about one dollar a day in extra tips. You know, a cab driver will give you a little 'smoosh' and you feel compelled to give him a little extra. Then there are the autograph hounds. I don't mind the well-behaved ones, but I abhor all those juvenile delinquents who descend upon you and shout, 'Who are you? Sign here!' "

By 1953, when the collection of Nash verse entitled *The Private Dining Room* was published, a reviewer stated, "He is unchallenged as the leading American writer of humorous verse. He probably is the most quoted of contemporary American poets, with a larger and more appreciative audience than any other poet."

Nash once suggested that the popularity of his work in Britain may stem from the fact that, being dismissed from the tradition of English poetry, he is enjoyed simply as an American exhibition. He thinks of his poetry as being so American as to be untranslatable, yet recent experience indicates he is overly modest.

On June 7, 1965, Theodore Shabad of *The New York Times* reported from Moscow concerning a program in which a Russian actor recited Nash's verse. Shabad wrote: "Vyacheslav Somov, professional reciter, had a full house in Sovetskaya concert hall, predominantly young listeners, and Nash's were perhaps the most popular of the works included in a 2½-hour program." Special favorites of the audience were "The Terrible People" ("people who have what they want and are very fond of telling people who haven't that they don't really want it") and "Golly How Truth Will Out" ("How does a person get to be a capable liar? / That is something I respectfully inquiar"), which, Shabad wrote, "seemed to lose nothing in translation and to surmount political and ideological differences."

In the 1950s, Ogden Nash began the first of his considerable contribution to children's literature, but he was careful to explain that "this writing is perhaps not wholly for children, but rather belongs in a 'twilight world' of both children and adults." He reserves the right not to write down or to underrate the intelligence of children, because, he says, "They like a good mouthful of words. I found I had been writing for children, so I thought I'd try doing it deliberately. I may have been writing for the 12-year-old mind all these years without knowing it."

In these volumes, such as the *Custard, the Dragon* books, there is the theme of truth set forth in delightful form; this is perhaps best illustrated by Nash's characteristic whimsical-serious approach to the young, as revealed in three examples of Nash insight:

He conceded poetically that "being a father / is quite a bother / but I like it, rather," and he once remarked to a Boston audience honoring him as winner of the city's Arts Festival poetry prize, "Oh adolescence, oh adolescence, I wince before thy incandescence." And the same man once recalled soberly that he watched a 5-year-old teetering on the roof of a farm building, and asked, "What are you doing up there?" "Trying not to fall off," the child said, implying that anyone with common sense should have perceived that. "It struck me," said Nash, "that that is what we are all trying to do—simply trying not to fall off."

In 1965, Nash found New York, after thirteen years, "too depressing and too expensive . . . $12 for a bunch of lilies of the valley," and returned to Baltimore, where he had lived for twenty years previously. Then working on his fifteenth volume of poetry, he remarked, "Every time I write another book, I figure I've got to give the public about three years to recover from my last one."

The range and sprightliness of Nash's humor are awesome —once he even wrote lyrics for a television show, "Peter and the Wolf," including a love song sung by a nearsighted dog to a duck, under the impression that she was a water spaniel. But his interviewers have often received "an impression of shyness and brooding sensitivity," and his more recent poetic observations reveal some of the things he thinks about in more serious moments.

He has said, "I like to think that beyond my work, there is a consistent individual point of view toward life, something

96

more than just jokes and odd rhymes." His viewpoint is: "This is our world, and we are locked in it. We have to learn to survive, whether we love or admire each other or not."

Asked by Hal Boyle of the Associated Press if he thought any of his verse had produced any enduring good for the human race, Nash, basically unpretentious, smiled and nominated the following lines, probably the most widely reprinted of all those he has written:

"I think that I shall never see / A billboard lovely as a tree / Perhaps unless the billboards fall / I'll never see a tree at all."

Speaking in the Library of Congress auditorium, an appearance sponsored by the Gertrude Clark Whittal Poetry and Literature Fund, Nash submitted that the average man, facing the perils of the nuclear age, needs not only missiles, submarines, and a fallout shelter to save him, but also "a few lighthearted laughs."

Again, at Pembroke College, he told his audience that he was worried because he did not see any young humorous writers on the horizon. He said, "At the time when we need it most, I don't see anybody coming along who is a writing humorist. Our writers all want to write Greek tragedy. Television and advertising have snapped up many bright young people because they pay more for their talents.

"Unfortunately, they also wear them out quickly, but I hope some of them emerge unscathed."

That's the kind of thing that's being done all the time by poets
    from Homer to Tennyson;
They're always comparing ladies to lilies and veal to venison.
And they always say things like that the snow is a white blanket
    after a winter storm.

Oh it is, is it, all right then, you sleep under a six-inch blanket of
  snow and I'll sleep under a half-inch blanket of unpoetical
  blanket material
And we'll see which one keeps warm.

Rhymed Treatise on Metaphors

DOROTHY PARKER

[1893–1967]

IN 1951, Dorothy Parker said she had given up writing verse "because I found I was getting no better at it." She added, with typical Parkerian wryness, "This magnificent gesture went unnoticed, I may say. No one clamored for a new group of Parker cute sayings in rhyme.

"Of course, I should like to write decent, durable prose. I should like, above all, to write a play—I mean a good play that says something. I can't so far."

This statement offers a clue to everything that Dorothy Parker was—a talented poet and short story writer, an expert in the often barbed witty remark, a writer of lesser known plays, a professional precisionist, and a woman of deep feeling.

Once called the wittiest woman of her generation, she also may have been one of the most misunderstood, for, in retrospect, her sharp-edged humor appears as a mask for the intense, passionate, and often melancholy spirit that she really was.

Her friend Alexander Woollcott once wrote, "She is a blend of Little Nell and Lady Macbeth. Her outward social manners are calculated to confuse the unwary and unnerve even those most addicted to the incomparable boon of her company. Her most effective vein is that of dispraise. Indeed, disparagement is so habitual to Mrs. Parker that she has no technique for praise and when she feels admiration, she can find no words for it."

Woollcott recalled that she once said to a departing guest, "I was terribly glad to see you. Do let me call you up sometime, won't you please?"

Born Dorothy Rothschild, the daughter of a New Yorker of means and a Scottish mother (who died when Dorothy was still an infant), in West End, New Jersey, she attended Miss Dana's School at Morristown, New Jersey, and the Sacred Heart Convent in New York. She later described herself as a "plain disagreeable child with stringy hair and a yen to write poetry."

When it became necessary, after her father's death, for her to earn money, she sent one of her poems to Frank Crowninshield, editor of the magazine *Vanity Fair*. Impressed by it, he obtained a job for her, writing picture captions for the fashion magazine *Vogue*, at $10 a week. At the same time, Franklin Pierce Adams, then writing his column "The Conning Tower" for the New York *Daily Mail*, published some of her tragicomic poetry.

She worked for *Vogue* for two years, 1916 and 1917; in the latter year, she married Edwin Pond Parker 2d, whom she had known for a long time, a week before his Army division sailed for France.

"After an interminable time," she recalled later, "and so long ago that women's parts in plays were taken by men," she became drama critic for *Vanity Fair*, holding that post from 1917 to 1920. Her departure came "during an office reorganization," according to *The New York Times*, although Mr. Woollcott wrote in 1936 that "she was removed from the post forcibly upon the bitter complaint of sundry wounded people of the theater."

Whichever version is more accurate, Dorothy Parker will be long remembered for having written of actress Katharine Hepburn, then appearing on Broadway in *The Lake*, "She runs the gamut of emotions from A to B." And of Channing Pollock's *The House Beautiful*, she concluded after the opening, "*The House Beautiful* is the play lousy."

During her *Vanity Fair* period, Dorothy Parker formed a lifetime association with a group of noted writers that included Woollcott, Robert Benchley, Robert E. Sherwood, Heywood Broun, Edna Ferber, Franklin Pierce Adams, and Harold Ross, founder and editor of *The New Yorker* magazine. Approximately ten of these congenial spirits lunched each day at the Algonquin Hotel Round Table, and Miss Parker soon gained a reputation, both deserved and otherwise, for her spontaneous and cutting wit.

Just how the legend began that, in the words of Willa Martin of the Associated Press, she "carried a dagger beneath her gay lacy gloves," is something of a mystery. Perhaps the late O. O. McIntyre, New York newspaper columnist, was responsible to a major degree. Though they never met, he quoted her regularly as a member of the Algonquin group; for that matter, so did her friends, including Dashiell Hammett, Benchley, and Charles MacArthur, playwright and husband of actress Helen Hayes, who often related the newest Parkerism.

In later years, Dorothy Parker remarked ruefully: "It is ridiculous to have such a reputation for quips. I am not witty and I am not funny. I say hardly any of those clever things that are attributed to me. I wouldn't have time to earn a living if I said all those things." She also came to feel that her reputation for being a lethal wit plagued her socially and professionally, that people fled from her because they feared her agile tongue, and that her more serious writing efforts suffered because she was known primarily as a quipster.

But her reputation for the bitter-sweet bon mot is well established and does not rely for confirmation upon hearsay or the remarks attributed to her by friends. This talented woman, described by Alden Whitman of *The New York Times* as "little, with dollish face and basset hound eyes, in whose mouth butter hardly ever melted," became a contributor to *The New Yorker* magazine from its second issue, February 28, 1925, until December 14, 1957. During this period, she produced ten volumes of verse, ranging from *Enough Rope* to *Sunset Gun*, and several outstanding short stories, including "Big Blonde," which won the O. Henry Memorial Award in 1929.

In her conversation, for she was much in demand at parties and literary gatherings, and in her book reviews for *The New Yorker* and later for *Esquire* magazine, Dorothy Parker's devastating comment, coupled with bone-bare truth, constantly reduced the mighty, left professional prestige in shreds, and greatly amused the multitudes.

As an example, in reviewing an autobiography, she wrote, "The affair between Margot Asquith and Margot Asquith will live as one of the prettiest love stories in all literature." In another review, she commented, "The reading of *Dawn* [by Theodore Dreiser] is a strain upon many parts, but the worst wear and tear fall on the forearms."

For *The New Yorker*, she reviewed books under the pseudonym "Constant Reader," and once irritated by A. A. Milne's use of the word "tummy" instead of stomach, dealt author and book a wicked blow by writing, "Tonstant Weader fwowed up."

In 1928, she was granted a divorce from Edwin Parker, although she retained his name professionally throughout her life. In 1933, she married Alan Campbell, an actor from Virginia, who eventually left his stage career to become a successful writer, on occasion collaborating with her on motion-picture scenarios.

Dorothy Parker's writing for stage and screen—although she is not as well known for this aspect of her career—covered several years and included a considerable body of work. In 1924, she and playwright Elmer Rice collaborated on a drama, *Close Harmony*, which was praised by the critics but was a failure financially.

During the next several years, some of her poignant short stories were presented as a program of playlets, and in 1949 she collaborated with Ross Evans on a play, *The Coast of Illyria*. This drama was named after the shore on which Viola and her twin brother, Sebastian, are shipwrecked in Shakespeare's *Twelfth Night*. Its plot was based on the life of Charles Lamb, English essayist and critic, and his sister Mary. The play was well received, but it never reached Broadway.

Though she did considerable writing for the movies, Dorothy Parker often said she did not like Hollywood; between scenarios, she returned to the literary world of New York or to her 111-acre farm in Bucks County, Pennsylvania. She once said, "I want nothing from Hollywood but money, and anyone who tells you that he came here [to Hollywood] for anything else or tries to make beautiful words out of it lies in his teeth."

She who wrote the famous lines "Men seldom make passes

/ At girls who wear glasses" had second thoughts about what was probably her most quoted couplet. In 1951, she told Bob Thomas of the Associated Press, "I rue the day that I wrote those lines more than any in my life. I wish I had the power to destroy them forever. It is a terrible thing to have made a serious attempt to write verse and then be remembered for two lines like those.

"In the first place, it is bad verse and in the second place, it isn't true. Women can look very attractive in glasses. I saw a pair the other day that were brightly colored, with little rhinestones like daisies all around the rims. But I am constantly plagued by those lines. I fear that couplet is going to follow me to my grave."

The products of Dorothy Parker's wit were by no means always cruel; they often concerned themselves candidly and somewhat exuberantly with life's absurd aspects or its inequities. One of the best-known examples of her cleverness without malice was a portion of conversation with the English novelist W. Somerset Maugham, who had been seated next to her at a dinner party.

Mr. Maugham asked her if she would write a poem for him. She said she would, and wrote hastily: "Higgledy piggledy, my white hen / She lays eggs for gentlemen." At that point, Maugham said he always had liked those lines. Dorothy Parker smiled, and without hesitation continued: "You cannot persuade her with gun or lariat / To come across for the proletariat."

In the foreword to one of Miss Parker's volumes of poetry, Maugham wrote: "However lyrical her mood, and when she likes, she can be as lyrical as Herrick and Landor at their charming best, her aerial flight is anchored to this pendant world (the phrase is Milton's) by the golden chain of common sense and what is it but common sense that makes this uncertain, absurd, harsh and transitory life not only tolerable, but amusing?"

The most superficial examination of her work bears out the truth of this statement. Thus, it was Dorothy Parker who remarked, "As far as I am concerned, the most beautiful word in the English language is cellar door; it was also she who remarked, "Salary is no object; I want only enough to keep body and soul apart."

Her verse, at once clever and cynical, half sentiment and half wryness, dealt often with the idea that romance must end in disenchantment. Typical is this quatrain: "Oh, life is a glorious cycle of song / A medley of extemporanea / And love is a thing that can never go wrong / And I am Marie of Roumania."

Dorothy Parker was a painstaking craftsman; she did not write nearly so rapidly as she spoke and thought. Ogden Nash, also a careful phrase polisher, once commented: "To say Miss Parker writes well is as fatuous as proclaiming that Cellini [16th-century Italian goldsmith and sculptor] was clever with his hands." She worked hard at writing, but, since her output was in great demand, was often delinquent in meeting publishers' deadlines.

Her definition of humor reveals how complex is the effort to make something appear funny, yet uncontrived: "Humor to me, heaven help me, takes in many things. There must be courage; there must be no awe. There must be criticism, for humor, to my mind, is encapsulated in criticism. There must be a disciplined eye and a wild mind. There must be a magnificent disregard of your reader, for if he cannot follow you, there is nothing you can do about it."

And she acknowledged that humor so demandingly defined did not come easily to the pen. "I can't write five words but that I change seven," she confessed. Of her poetry, she added, "I was following in the exquisite footsteps of Miss Edna St. Vincent Millay, unhappily, in my own horrible sneakers." Even if she had not said this, the bitter-sweet truths characteristic of Millay's writing can also be discovered in such Parker lines as these: "Soldier in a curious land / All across a swaying sea / Take her smile and lift her hand / Have no guilt of me."

Whatever she may have thought of Hollywood, she returned there many times to collaborate on movie scenarios, including *Here Is My Heart, The Big Broadcast of 1936, Lady Be Careful, A Star Is Born, Sweethearts, Trade Winds,* and *Saboteur.*

She contributed lyrics to Leonard Bernstein's musical, "Candide," and made a last attempt at playwriting in 1953, collaborating on *Ladies of the Corridor* with Arnaud d'Usseau. This was a story concerned with the aimless and empty lives of a group of aged and aging women who lived in a New York residential hotel. The play had a moderately successful Broadway run.

In the spring of 1963, in her 70th year, Dorothy Parker was living in Hollywood. There, an interviewer noted her "black-gray hair in bangs, her mouth in a small-girl smile, her big round brown eyes in a look of startled innocence." (She had a black French poodle, named Cliché because, she explained, "the streets are carpeted with black French poodles.")

At that time, she was having a brief fling at teaching courses in the American and English novel at Los Angeles State College. She observed: "It is hard work. The only real reward is the two or three students you find who are alive and responsive and worth all the trouble." She found the new college generation "more interested in education than mine was." (She once said, "The only thing I ever learned in school that did me any good in after life was that if you spit on a pencil eraser, it will erase ink.")

But she also thought present-day youth seemed to be "more puritanical, if you can imagine that, and less adventuresome. There is not much dissent. I have counted only three beards out of a student body of at least 18,000."

Moreover, she was struck by the lack of humor in the young. She said, "They can't blame it all on the bomb. They can't worry about it all the time. Why don't they laugh?" Even among adults, she concluded. "There just aren't any humorists today. I don't suppose there is much demand for humor. S. J. Perelman is about the only one working at it, and he's rewriting himself."

Later, in 1963, her husband and collaborator, Alan Campbell, died, after which, having lived in Hollywood for fourteen years, Miss Parker, already ill, moved back to New York. She wanted to resume writing but lacked the energy, and, in her last years, became melancholy about her professional accomplishments.

From the late 1920s, when she was fined $5 for "sauntering" in a Boston demonstration against the execution of Nicola Sacco and Bartolomeo Vanzetti, Dorothy Parker was active in liberal causes. During the Spanish civil war and afterward, she was national chairman of the Joint Anti-Fascist Refugee Committee and active in its behalf.

In 1951, she was cited by the House Un-American Activities Committee, with 300 other writers, professors, actors, and artists, for affiliation with what the Committee designated as "communist-front" organizations. One Committee witness identified her as a member of the Communist party, an accusation that she persistently denied.

She left no survivors, and bequeathed the bulk of her estate to the Reverend Dr. Martin Luther King, civil rights leader, whom she had apparently never met. At her funeral, Lillian Hellman, the playwright, and Zero Mostel, the actor, delivered the eulogies.

Of Dorothy Parker's contribution to American literature, critic Edmund Wilson has said, "She is not Emily Brontë or Jane Austen, but she has been at some pains to write well, and she has put into what she has written a voice, a state of mind, an era, a few moments of human experience that nobody else has conveyed."

> A single flow'r he sent me, since we met,
> All tenderly his messenger he chose;
> Deep-hearted, pure, with scented dew still wet—
> One perfect rose.
>
> . . . . .
>
> Why is it no one ever sent me yet
> One perfect limousine, do you suppose?
> Ah, no, it's always just my luck to get
> One perfect rose.

JAMES WHITCOMB RILEY

[1849-1916]

In the files of the New Bedford Massachusetts *Standard-Times*, there is a fragile, yellowed newspaper clipping dated October 8, 1898, and identified as an autobiographical sketch of James Whitcomb Riley. Written in the third person, it reveals that he was born at Greenfield, Indiana, and goes on to say: "He was ill-starred from the very cradle, it appears. One day, while but a toddler, he climbed, unseen, to an open window, where some potted flowers were ranged.

"Then, while leaning from his high chair far out, to catch some dainty gilded butterfly, perchance, he lost his footing and, with a piercing shriek, fell headlong to the graveled walk below, and when, an instant later, the affrighted parents picked him up—he was a poet.

"The father of young Riley was a lawyer of large practice who used, in moments of deep thought, to regard his boy as the worst case he ever had. This may have been the reason that, in time, he insisted on his reading law, which the boy really tried to do; but finding that political economy and Blackstone didn't rhyme, he slid out of the office one hot, sultry afternoon and ran away with a patent medicine and concert wagon, from the tail end of which he was discovered by some relatives of his in the next town, violently abusing a bass drum.

"Fortunately, in former years, he had purloined some knowledge of a trade. He could paint a sign—or a house—or a tin roof—if someone else would furnish him the paint—and one of Riley's hand-painted picket fences was a rapture to the most exacting eye. . . .

"He made friends and money, too, enough at last to gratify the highest ambition of his life, namely, to own an overcoat with fur around the tail of it. Eventually, he took his sappy paragraphs and poetry to another town and another paper and there did better, till he spoilt it all by devising a Poe poem fraud, by which he lost his job and in disgrace and humiliation shoe-mouth deep, his feelings gave way beneath his feet and his heart broke with a loud report. So the true poet was born. . . .

"Speaking coyly of himself one day, he said, 'I write from the heart; that's one good thing I like about me. I may not write a good hand and my copy may occasionally get mixed up with the market reports, but all the same, what challenges my admiration is that humane peculiarity of mine, i.e., writing from the heart and, therefore, to the heart."

Although written lightly, this is a poignant sketch of the warmth, humor, and heartache that characterized the life of an outstandingly successful American poet who has been criticized for Victorian sentimentality, manufactured dialect, and out-of-focus child characters, but whose popularity among children continues.

His first verses were published when he was 34; in ten years, more than 500,000 copies had been sold, and new volumes appeared annually until there were at least 44 first editions. "Little Orphant Annie," "The Raggedy Man," and

"Nine Little Goblins," probably his best-known verses, from time to time are dismissed by editors of anthologies, but youngsters still memorize them in school, fractured English and all, and ask for them at libraries.

The odd thing about this is that Riley, who had no children, undoubtedly was writing for adults about the carefree and somewhat romanticized days gone by, but it is the young people themselves who continue to like what he has to say.

Even with the perspective of time, it is difficult to understand how Riley, who ran away from home at 18, attained such literary heights that the Associated Press said of him, a year before his death, "The world was so touched by his inspiration and the realism of his homely symbols that he was one of the few that, devoting their lives to poetry, gained a fortune."

By contrast, academicians today more often than not suggest that James Whitcomb Riley, who never felt at home beyond the boundaries of his native Indiana, actually excluded realism from his writings and dealt with a misty, secure world of childhood that never existed, and which, moreover, was in direct contrast to the massive new awakenings of a growing nineteenth-century America.

He was the son of Reuben A. Riley, a lawyer and political speaker; his mother was Elizabeth Marine Riley, a writer of verse, and the poet in later life attributed some of his "impracticability" to her.

Instead of preparing for the practice of law as his father wished, the son became an itinerant sign painter. For ten years, he roved the Ohio Valley, applying his knack with brush and pencil to the painting of advertising signs and sketches. An Associated Press writer later reported: "He was naturally musical and shone as a fiddler in the villages at which his party stopped at night. He played for dances and at concerts in country hotels. He wrote rhymes that sometimes found their way into country newspapers."

Riley ended this cheerful, free-and-easy life in 1877, when he took a job as reporter for a newspaper in Anderson, Indiana. It was here that he perpetrated the "Poe hoax" which, as his secretary, J. M. Dickey, said years later, brought the poet his first recognition beyond Indiana. The verse involved was titled "Leonanie"; it was offered to the public as a hitherto unpublished poem of Edgar Allan Poe, who had died in 1849. It read, in part: "Leonanie, angels named her / And they took the light / Of the laughing stars and framed her / In a smile of white."

In some quarters, the poem was accepted as genuine; in others, it was denounced as a fraud; the controversy raged for months until Riley confessed his authorship.

In the early eighties, Riley began writing verses in "Hoosier dialect" for the Indianapolis *Journal*. Controversy continues to this day as to whether any residents of Indiana actually spoke in this manner, or whether it was a literary invention. Others of the period, including Bret Harte, were making effective use of dialect to portray the unlettered provincial as a person of shrewdness and compassion.

Riley sent some of his verses to Henry Wadsworth Longfellow, whom he admired greatly, and received that famous poet's praise. A volume was published and "the Hoosier poet" began to win a public. He was an excellent reader of his dialect verse, and for fifteen years, or until 1898, he made nationwide tours with great success, appearing in public with his intimate friend, the humorist Bill Nye. The picture bequeathed to us by his contemporaries is that of a neatly dressed man, warm in manner and fond of children, clad in an immaculate and tightly buttoned frock coat, and wearing rimmed reading glasses, from which a black cord dangles.

Longfellow died when Riley was in his early thirties, but shortly before that event, the Hoosier poet visited him in Cambridge. Recalling their conversation, Riley commented: "The world, Mr. Longfellow said, was teeming with beautiful themes for the versifier; they could never be exhausted. This gave me a great light as to his methods. I understood then, as indeed I had before vaguely surmised, that he always saw the poetic in that which was nearest to him; that he made constant use of what we often called the commonplace."

The Canadian poet Bliss Carman (to whom Riley dedicated his volume *Songs o' Cheer*) and the eminent author-editor William Dean Howells considered Riley "the greatest American poet of our generation," according to a newspaper article written by poet Joyce Kilmer in 1916.

Bliss Carman said: "I remember Riley as very deliberate in his motions, especially in his last years. Smooth shaven, ruddy, well groomed, he looked like a benign old English bishop.

"Riley was at the Hotel Walton in Philadelphia, having his portrait painted by John Singer Sargent. I went to Philadelphia to read before the Browning Society. After the reading was over, Riley tucked me under his arm and said, 'Now let's get around to the hotel and we'll take off our shoes and get a chew of tobacco and be comfortable.'

"You know, such remarks as this were all the more piquant because Riley was so very punctilious and scrupulous in all his personal habits. He always was immaculately dressed. I never knew him even to make so much of a concession to comfort as to put on a smoking jacket or a lounge coat. But he liked to go to his room and stretch himself on his bed. And he never talked about anything but literature, chiefly poetry. Two poets to whom he was especially devoted were Longfellow and Swinburne; he liked Swinburne's music and deft craftsmanship.

"After Riley had received his degrees from some of the colleges [Yale, University of Pennsylvania, and Indiana University, among others, awarded him honorary degrees], he seemed to feel that he ought to be known as a poet, rather than as a humorist and a writer of dialect verse. He tried hard to live up to the name of poet and wanted his nonsense rhymes of his vagabondage forgotten. Yet his vernacular verse, or as he called it, his dialect verse, was his chief contribution to literature."

In 1893, Riley attended the World's Columbian Exposition in Chicago. It was "Indiana Day," and a newspaper reporter wrote: "On the right of the governor of the state stood Benjamin Harrison, ex-general, ex-United States senator and ex-president of the United States. Next in line to the president was an undersized, boyish man. His face was the personification of good nature, good humor and pathos and he was as happy as a schoolboy on the eventful occasion when school's out for the year.

"As the line came along, there were greetings and expressions of the greatest esteem and respect for Mr. Harrison, but everybody, man, woman and child, knew the little man, James Whitcomb Riley, by sight and called him by name. They shook his hand with characteristic cordiality as if they had known him always. The rich and the poor claimed him as their own."

On June 25, 1953, two years after the publication of a well-thought-of anthology of children's literature which concluded that the popularity of Riley's verses seemed to be waning, and nearly forty years after the poet's death, the Associated Press reported from Indianapolis:

"Even children get winded climbing the hill to James Whitcomb Riley's grave in Crown Hill Cemetery. Yet the famed Hoosier poet's resting place once more is the No. 1 attraction to visitors of Crown Hill, one of the nation's largest cemeteries. Here also are buried a president, three vice presidents, scores of people prominent in literature and industry, and the bank-robbing gang leader John H. Dillinger, shot down by federal agents in 1934.

" 'For a while, it used to be that Dillinger's grave was visited the most,' said Howard T. Wood, Crown Hill executive manager. 'Now, it's Riley again.' "

The public's idols come and go, but the man who wrote "Wunst we went a-fishing, me / And my pa and ma, all three" continues to play on the heartstrings of the young—and, obviously, of some of those older, too. A member of the American Academy of Arts and Letters, James Whitcomb Riley received the gold medal of the National Institute of Arts and Letters, and in 1915 his birthday, October 7, was declared an official holiday throughout his home state in honor of Indiana's "most beloved citizen."

Little Orphant Annie's come to our house to stay,
An' wash the cups and saucers up, and brush the crumbs away,
An' shoo the chickens off the porch, and dust the hearth, an'
    sweep,
An' make the fire, and bake the bread, an' earn her board-an'-
    keep;
An' all us other children, when the supper things is done,
We set around the kitchen fire an' has the mostest fun
A-list'nin' to the witch-tales 'at Annie tells about,
An' the Gobble-uns 'at gits you

Ef you
Don't
Watch
Out!
—*Little Orphant Annie*

BERT LESTON TAYLOR

[1866–1921]

BERT LESTON TAYLOR, known throughout most of his professional life as "B.L.T.," was a native of Goshen, Massachusetts, and was educated at the College of the City of New York, but the first indications of what he was to become emerged during his early newspaper career in Vermont.

He went to Montpelier in 1887, when he was 20, after a brief newspaper experience in Brattleboro, Vermont. Until 1893, he was employed most of the time as a reporter on the *Argus and Patriot,* described by those who remembered the publication as a "militant Democratic weekly."

After his death, Bert Taylor was remembered in Montpelier with exceptional fondness, not only for his sprightly humor in newspapering but also for his outstanding musical ability. Old friends recalled that he was a "live wire" in the Apollo Club, the leading social organization of Vermont's capital city, and especially so in the production of the major minstrel show it staged in the early 1890s.

One of the songs Taylor wrote for it, complete with local allusions, was entitled, "It Has Never Been Fully Explained." A verse of it related that "Old Noah he did build an ark / And started for a cruise / And all the other animals /

Walked in by twos and twos. / Now if a certain gentleman / Had been there in the swim / I wonder what in thunder / Would have walked along with him." Then the chorus, of course, went on to state, "It has never been fully explained."

During this period, Taylor also wrote at least three comic operas, which were purchased and produced by a Boston group then in its heyday, known as The Bostonians.

One of the musicals was *The Explorers*, which, according to contemporaries, may have set some kind of speed record, for it was written in thirty days, and thirty days thereafter the curtain rose on its first night at Boston's Tremont Theater. The principal feature of the show was a mastodon's "funny bone," which was endowed with the power to make people laugh when it was pointed at them to the accompaniment of the magic word "kapow."

The play also concerned an Iowa corn queen, Mazy Fields, whose picture floated ashore on a tropical island and inspired romantic notions in a savage chieftain. This is a sample of the B.L.T. libretto: "Oh, I'm an explorer / And I'm an adorer / Of everything novel and new / And all of the papers / Are full of my capers / They print everything that I do."

Much of Taylor's newspaper writing at this time was unsigned and appeared in a column of local happenings entitled "Montpelier Mere Mention" but those who knew him well have suggested that the following excerpts from "M.M.M." possess the unmistakable B.L.T. touch:

"There was a pleasant party in Berlin Block last week, somewhat of the same nature as the one held at the christening of the celebrated McSorley twins. A general knockdown and dragout was introduced, to which all present were invited. One of the combatants had one of the windows of his soul blacked, nearly knocking out the sash."

"Jumbo, the nine-year-old cat of Charles Wade, walked into the dining room of the home last Monday night after an absence of two years."

"Jack Connelly is suffering from a fractured finger caused by playing ball when the laws of God and man declared that he should not have been doing so."

One of the few signed articles by Taylor between 1887 and 1892 is the report of a "Jacksonian dinner," held in January, 1891, in Manchester, New Hampshire. After a summary of the speech-making, he ended his news account by writing: "About half past one, the company rose from the tables, gave three good Democratic cheers and went home to dream of an avalanche of ballots in 1892 that will bury the Republican Party so far under ground that it will never even sprout again."

Taylor published a newspaper briefly in Barre; called *The Town News*, this six-page venture expired on July 11, 1890, with an issue bearing the pathetic legend "Vol. 1, No. 15 and last."

In the column "Editorially Speaking," under the heading "Adios," Taylor stated, in part: "Owing to circumstances (and other parties) which have become uncontrollable, I feel it my duty to announce that *The Town News* this week ceases to illumine the literary and journalistic atmosphere of America and Barre. . . .

"I should like to continue to live in Barre . . . but metaphysicians have demonstrated that wind, as an article of diet, is not conducive to longevity . . . and that soft answers never butter any parsnips. So farewell, Barre. . . ."

Moving west after his marriage to Emma Bonner of Providence, Rhode Island, in 1895, Taylor worked for Duluth newspapers for several years, and in 1899 joined the staff of the Chicago *Journal*. Its editor one day commented that many unusual items published in rural newspapers would, if effectively collected and presented, make a readable column; he asked all the reporters to watch for such items. Long familiar with the small-town press, Taylor did the best job of "collecting and presenting," and was assigned to write an editorial-page column to be called "A Little About Everything."

Two years later, he joined the staff of the Chicago *Tribune*. There he started the column that was to become famous, "A Line o' Type or Two," concerning which he punned: "Hew to the Line; let the quips fall where they may." In a year or two, as a contemporary has noted, both his column and his initials had become "national monuments."

Taylor resigned from the *Tribune* in 1903 to go to New York, where for six years he was one of the editors of *Puck* magazine and a contributor to the New York *Sun*. In 1909, however, he returned to Chicago and resumed the "Line." He is credited with the discovery, encouragement, and guidance of F.P.A. (Franklin Pierce Adams), who attained equal fame as the conductor of a newspaper column. F.P.A. was originally one of B.L.T.'s contributors, one of the multitude from all walks of life whose offerings made the "Line's" daily mail voluminous.

Readers throughout the world came to know "B.L.T.," as Taylor signed his column, and addressed mail to him by those initials. His legions of followers and armies of contributors regarded him with rare affection. To "make the Line" was regarded as a signal honor, not only by the obscure, but by men and women already famed as poets and authors. Under such pseudonyms as Pan, Riquarius, and Anchusa, the distinguished won a double fame—perhaps more titillating because it was anonymous—with their contributions to Taylor's column.

The volume of these contributions and the intellectual level of many who offered them attest to the fact that B.L.T. was not simply a columnist or a "funny man," but much more, including a cultured social satirist. His bright sayings, syndicated in many other daily newspapers, were quoted by thousands as, during his 20 years as author and editor, his stature continued to increase—not in a single category, but as humorist, journalist, poet, and man of letters.

In addition to his column, the publishing of such Taylor works as *The Well in the Wood* (1904); *The Charlatans* (1906); *A Line o' Verse or Two* (1911); *The Pipesmoke Carry* (1912), and *Motley Measures* (1913) revealed the merit of his verse and the depth of his acquaintance with good literature. It is of significance that in 1919 a dinner was given in Boston in his honor, at which President Ernest Martin Hopkins of Dartmouth College, former Assistant Secretary of the Treasury Louis A. Coolidge, and others testified to the literary value of and the popular interest in Taylor's writings.

It was his pride and his paper's that, after the first years of the "Line," B.L.T. became independent of all editorial supervision. Often "A Line o' Type or Two" disagreed with other columns on the editorial page. At one time, Taylor even carried on a mild campaign in ridicule of his newspaper colleagues' defense of "It's me" and "It don't," as phrases in common usage. "Flubdub," to use his own term—that is to say, mushy thinking—he assailed at every turn, comparing it to that mushiest of all American institutions, bread pudding, which he also disliked intensely.

What Bert Taylor was is revealed in the comments of

those who, on March 28, 1921, were among the hundreds
from all stations of life who paid public tribute to him in
Chicago's Blackstone Theater nine days after his death at the
age of 56.

Death had come most unexpectedly. His readers, early in
March of that year, became aware through his whimsical
comments in the "Line" that B.L.T. had bronchitis. For a
few days, there were blithely dismal comments on the mis-
eries of such afflictions. Mr. Taylor discovered an advertisement in a small Wisconsin newspaper, in which a typo-
graphical error caused a farmer to announce that he had "a
three-year-old cold for sale," and, in his next to last column,
B.L.T. commented, "We have one we will dispose of at a
sacrifice, and throw in a prescription line."

But the illness was far more serious than had been assumed
at first, and Mr. Taylor died of pneumonia with a suddenness
that shocked his friends and followers.

Some have suggested that Taylor's posthumously published *The So-Called Human Race* sums up what he thought
of his fellow men; yet this conclusion takes into account
neither the compassion expressed in his writings nor the Chicago plasterer, who said he never had met B.L.T., but had
"made the Line" three times, and sacrificed a day's wages to
attend Mr. Taylor's funeral.

Surely there is no misanthropy in such lines as these:

"Am I inspired to mirth or mockery / Grant, spirit, that it
not be overdrawn / And am I moved to malice, let it be /
Only 'the sunny malice of a faun.' "

At the Blackstone ceremonies, Taylor's eulogists portrayed
his many facets. Karleton S. Hackett, former president of
Chicago's American Conservatory of Music, noted that Mr.

Taylor's mind "was an alembic in which banalities—'flub-dub'—dissolved, and yet so simply, so inevitably, that there was no sediment of bitterness left behind, but what there was of truth or wit came forth purged . . . There was in his nature something shy, aloof, that found itself most at home out in the open, under the great pines."

Acknowledging his professional indebtedness, Franklin Pierce Adams wrote, "When with your gentle hand you showed a faltering, but adoring youth the road . . . sweet friend . . . Light is my threnody and crude / I might have made it heavier, were it / Not that I knew this is how you'd prefer it."

Horace J. Bridges recalled this episode: "Some three years ago in his column, B.L.T. said something to the effect that the third stanza of Keats' 'Ode on a Grecian Urn' would have been much better if Keats had worked longer over it. I thought he was joking, and under this impression I perpetrated a parody of it, which he printed. But in a subsequent conversation, he told me that his remark was serious.

"It is a fact that the third stanza is very inferior to the rest of that bewilderingly beautiful poem. Thus is some light thrown on Taylor; his work seldom betrayed the lack of that extra concentration, the difference between the good and excellent."

Author Henry Kitchell Webster said of Bert Leston Taylor: "The beginning of his art was a fastidious sensitiveness to words. They lived for him; they were as individual as his words which could be precise, without being pretentious. He friends. He loved the bold, outspoken, clean-edged ones, was no snob about them. Many an impudent, new-hatched gamin of a word that came grinning to him from the streets . . . he welcomed with wholehearted joy and introduced among the grandees of his vocabulary. . . .

"His two volumes of verse would entitle him to rank as a poet and a good one . . . His writings were a pinch of Attic salt. . . ."

In complimenting B.L.T.'s verse, Webster undoubtedly had in mind such varied offerings, both whimsical and thoughtful, as these:

"Everywhere I look I see / Fact or fiction, life or play, / Still the little game of Three: / B and C in love with A."

And of the wearisome weight of the daily burden: "When quacks with pills political would dope us, / When politics absorbs the livelong day, / I like to think about the star Canopus, / So far, so far away!"

Taylor was fond of stars, as he was of "the great pines" and all the world of nature. In "The Road to Anywhere," he wrote, "And when the fragrant day is done, / Night—and a shoal of stars."

He once commented, "When I am bidden to the journey through the narrow vale, I hope the message will come, not in the summer, but in the spring, the season of birth in death."

And so it was.

> Where (as ballades so oft begin)
> The classic clowns of yesterday?
> Where Guillaume of the famous grin,
> And eke the gifted Gaultier?
> And Tabarin, whose equine-play
> Appealed to foreheads high and steep?
> Gentles, we hand them this bouquet:
> It was to laugh and not to weep.
> —*Ballade of Old-Time Clowns*

INDEX

125

INDEX